An Eye for an Eye

Peter and Connie Roop

JAMESTOWN PUBLISHERS

a division of NTC/CONTEMPORARY PUBLISHING GROUP
Lincolnwood, Illinois USA

Especially for John, Marty, Maren, Emily, and Marta—
All roads lead to Williamsburg and Monticello.

Cover Credits
  Design: Herman Adler Design Group
  Illustration: David Schweitzer
  Timeline: (left) The Granger Collection; (middle) Library of Congress;
  (right) North Wind

ISBN: 0-8092-0587-4 (hardbound)
ISBN: 0-8092-0628-5 (softbound)

Published by Jamestown Publishers,
a division of NTC/Contemporary Publishing Group, Inc.,
4255 West Touhy Avenue,
Lincolnwood (Chicago), Illinois 60712-1975 U.S.A.

4 5 6 7 8 9 10 11 12 045 08 07 06 05 04 03 02 01

Chesapeake Bay Area 1776

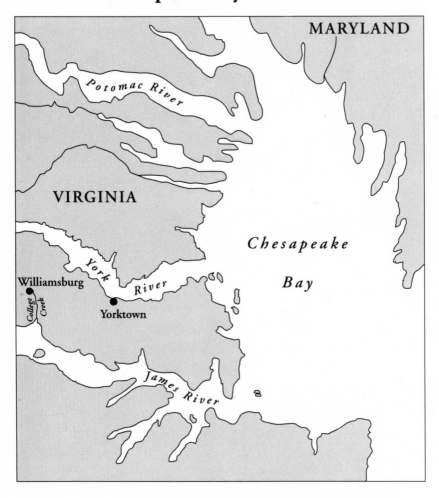

Chapter 1

Samantha raised her musket. Closing her left eye, she sighted down the long barrel. Her enemy stood statue still, his red coat a perfect target.

She aimed for his heart.

She drew a breath and held it as her finger gently squeezed the trigger.

Sensing danger, the fox turned his head. His black eyes bored into Samantha's. Neither blinked.

Hounds bayed near College Creek. The fox's scent was fresh. The hunt was on.

Samantha relaxed her finger and lowered her gun. The fox, a red flash, disappeared into the Virginia forest.

"Sam, why in tarnation didn't you shoot?" cried James. "That fox raids Mama's henhouse. 'Tis your duty to shoot it."

Samantha looked at her twin. They both had the same

color green eyes, which flashed when they angered. *So alike*, she thought, *yet so different*. She flicked a runaway strand of red hair back from her face.

"Why didn't *you* shoot?" she asked.

They both knew the answer. Samantha could outshoot James whether they hunted raccoon, turkey, fox, or deer. James couldn't hit the side of a tobacco shed from 50 feet.

Samantha gazed at the spot where the fox had stood. In the early morning light she imagined it still standing there, daring her to shoot. Why hadn't she pulled the trigger, sending the musket ball into its red fur? Because the fox was free and she wanted it to have a chance. Besides, gunpowder was too precious to waste on an unnecessary shot. Yes, she hunted to put food on the table and to provide game to sell in Williamsburg. And to stop varmints from raiding the henhouse. That was one thing. But to hunt for the sake of having something to do was another thing altogether.

Samantha disliked Thomas Wormley and his Tory friends who hunted for sport. Their wealth, built on the backs of slaves and indentured servants like her great-great-grandfather Richard Ayre, galled her.

And now Tories and Patriots threatened to shoot each other. How could people kill each other? She could never shoot someone. Throughout the colonies, people spoke of war against England. Spoke like it was going to be a pleasant outing.

Samantha felt her life was good. She had family and food. Of course, she had chores to do: weeding the garden, washing, cooking meals, collecting eggs, milking the cow, mending clothes, spinning thread. But when these chores were finished, Papa allowed her the freedom to roam the woods and sail the creeks.

Why go to war over a few pennies a pound for tea?

Samantha tucked the wayward strand of hair under her cap again. "Come on, James. Let's see if we can scare up a turkey to replace the hen Mama lost last night."

"But, Sam," James protested.

Samantha didn't answer. Instead, she bent under a dogwood tree branch.

"Wait, Sam. I want to take some snakeroot to Mama. Her medicines are running low," James called.

"You stay there until I come back," Samantha ordered patiently.

She stopped in a shadow as her older brother Henry had taught her. She paused, listening to the awakening forest. Cardinals chirped. Their companions answered. Squirrels rattled leaves looking for hidden nuts. A bobwhite called cheerily, "Bob white. Bob white." Samantha whistled an answering call, mimicking the bird perfectly.

As still as a tree trunk, Samantha listened and looked. Then she disappeared—like the fox—into the shadows, her hair a red flash.

The hunting hounds, still on the fox's trail, bayed.

She hoped to shoot a tasty turkey before James got too helplessly lost. Samantha smiled at the thought. Henry, 18 years old and aching to cross the Proclamation Line into the frontier, had tried and tried to teach James the ways of the woods. James, instead, insisted on stopping constantly to pick and name every plant species he could find. Some he gave to Mama to make into powders and poultices for healing. Others he would dry and add to his collection of Virginia plants.

If only they had the money, Papa would send him to the College of William and Mary in Williamsburg, where he could study to his heart's delight. Maybe even become a doctor.

If only.

Samantha's life was run by if onlys. If only she would wear a dress. If only she could keep her temper. If only, if only, if only.

Papa was saving every penny to buy more land. There was not a penny to spare for college, especially with the threat of war shading every decision Papa made. He had an eye on a parcel of Thomas Wormley's land, if Wormley should sell it and leave for England. Samantha wondered why Wormley still stayed in Virginia when he favored the British so much and was against loyal Virginians like Papa and Henry. Maybe he would leave next year in 1776.

Samantha absorbed Henry's knowledge like a sun-parched field drinks rain. She could never have enough. Henry could foretell the weather by the smell of the wind. He could tell directions by watching the sun and stars. He tracked animals as if he were one of their kin. His burning desire was to go west across the mountains into the wilds of Kentucky. Samantha hoped to go with him, but Mama would not allow such talk.

"Samantha Byrd," Mama would say, "when will you stop skylarking, put on a skirt, and behave like a lady?"

"Someday," Samantha would answer out loud. *Never*, she would say in her head. Mama meant well, but Samantha enjoyed the freedom of dressing in breeches, like a man, rather than in skirts. Yet she was 14 going on 15. She could not hope to roam the woods and water forever.

When Samantha complained to Henry that she would never be as good in the woods as he was, he would reply, "But, Sam, you know the wind, waves, and water better than I'll ever know the woods. In a boat, I am like James." They both had laughed, picturing the clumsy James bumbling in a boat. He could give the Latin name of every fish Samantha caught, but he could not catch one, even if it was served to him steaming on a plate.

In her skiff, Samantha was an otter, gliding along the winding College Creek. She knew every bend, every inlet, every place where deer drank or fish leapt or ducks nested. She knew where the plumpest oysters lay. She could catch crabs where no one else could. Samantha was one with the water.

Samantha stopped suddenly. The hounds bayed. But in the underbrush ahead a bush stirred.

Grasping her gun in her left hand, she raised her right hand to her mouth.

"Gobble, gobble, gobble," she called.

No reply.

She called again. "Gobble, gobble, gobble."

No reply.

All at once a hand closed over her mouth.

"Don't make a sound," her assailant whispered.

Chapter 2

Samantha sunk her teeth into the hand. The grip immediately loosened.

"Samantha, you knucklehead. It's me, Henry. There are two turkeys just beyond that bush."

Samantha did not turn around. She stared at the bush, just able to make out the rounded shapes of the turkeys.

"Gobble, goooooble," Henry called. His turkey call sounded so real it was as if another turkey hid behind them.

The bush quivered. Two turkeys waddled out, feeding on the remnants of last year's bumper crop of acorns.

"I'll take the tom. You take the hen," Henry whispered.

Samantha raised her musket. It had to be a clean shot or the musket ball would ruin the meat. And she would waste a shot. With gunpowder as precious as silver, she could not afford to miss.

She breathed in, held her breath, and squeezed the trigger.

Fire flared as the spark from the flint exploded the gunpowder. The musket kicked back against her shoulder. A cloud of smoke blocked her view. Henry's gun went off a split second after hers.

Samantha ducked under the smoke to see one turkey lying on the ground. It was the tom.

"I missed," she hissed.

"Not by much," Henry consoled her, holding the bird by its feet. "We will have turkey for dinner. Take it home to Mama."

"But, Henry," Samantha asked. "Aren't you coming home now?"

"Later," he said, drawing a paper cartridge from the leather pouch hanging from his belt. "I have some business to attend to." He sucked on his finger where she had bitten him.

Samantha didn't even ask what business it was, although she knew it had something to do with the militia. Or the Sons of Liberty. She had overheard him talking with Papa about carrying messages to Patrick Henry.

Like her brother, Samantha reloaded her musket.

"Never be caught with your musket unloaded," he had warned her time and again. "You never know when you might need to shoot."

Sometimes, she forgot and missed some excellent game.

Samantha tore off the end paper with her teeth and spit it on the ground. Holding the musket barrel upright, she carefully poured powder and ball down the long neck. She tapped it down with the ramrod before pouring a capful of powder into the firing pan. She closed the cover to keep the powder from spilling.

"Tell Mama I'll be home for roast turkey," Henry said. He flashed a smile at Samantha, tousled her hat so her hair fell loose, and slipped into the woods.

Samantha watched him disappear before she turned back toward the dogwood where she had left James.

She walked through the forest, not even trying to be quiet. Burdened with the turkey and her musket, she couldn't carry any more game even it lay down dead at her feet.

When she reached the dogwood tree, she only half-expected James to be there. His musket leaned against a loblolly pine tree. His black hat was on the ground. The hunting hounds bayed, their cries louder.

"Where is he?" she exclaimed to the forest. She set the turkey down and looked around for James's tracks. She saw where he had broken a branch. She spied a trail of leaves leading west instead of east towards home.

He was heading straight toward the approaching foxhunt. Mr. Wormley would be furious if James ruined his hunt.

The hounds bayed as if picking up fresh scent. Samantha, dodging trees, raced along James's trail. Ahead she saw an opening where the woods ended and Wormley's tobacco fields began. The sound of the hounds was louder.

Samantha stopped, looked, and listened. Her eyes flitted from tree to tree. She hoped to see the fox again, but it had fled in the opposite direction. Unless it was playing a trick on the hunters, laying a scent one way and doubling back to throw the hounds off the trail.

Overhead the wind ran through the trees. *Straight from the southeast*, she thought. *With this wind behind me on an incoming tide, I could be in Williamsburg before noon if I was in my skiff. Tomorrow, I'll take my crabs and oysters . . .*

Samantha remembered that tomorrow was fair day. Market Square would be crowded with folks buying and selling everything from slaves to horses. "I'll earn a pretty penny," she whispered.

The cries of the hounds brought her back to the task at hand: finding wayward James. Gripping her musket, Samantha hurried to the forest's border. She hoped to pick up his tracks along the edge of the tobacco field. She squinted as she left the forest shadows. She surveyed half the field before riveting her eyes on the galloping hunters, who were veering toward her right.

There stood James, collecting rose hips.

Samantha melted back into the forest. The hounds bayed frantically as they headed straight for him.

Thomas Wormley raised his gun.

Chapter 3

Samantha saw the puff of smoke before she heard the crack of Wormley's gun. James swatted the air as if an angry bee was buzzing near him. Then he saw the horses heading his way. He dropped his plants and hightailed it toward the woods.

Samantha ran too, pushing branches out of her way and leaping over logs. She paused at the top of a ravine, the steep green slope sliding down to a stream at the bottom. The ravine was too deep to cross. It would take her too long to go around. She veered out of the forest, not caring now if Wormley saw her or not.

"James!" she yelled. Wormley and his friends couldn't hear her over the thunder of their horses' hooves. They still galloped toward James.

James ran into the woods.

Samantha stood still and listened. Something crashed through the forest, now on her right. She caught a glimpse of red. Not the fox, she hoped, for the dogs would soon catch its scent and come her way.

James ran weaving between the trees.

"Over here," Samantha cried, dodging into the forest. The hunters turned her way.

James, breathless, leaned against a tree. Samantha grabbed his arm and pulled him in.

"I can't," he whined.

"You must," she snarled. "If you don't keep running, Wormley will sic his hounds on you."

He resisted for a second longer and then gave in.

"We'll head for the dogwood. Follow me and don't fall behind."

The cries of the hounds gave James the energy he needed to keep pace with her.

As they struggled through the undergrowth, Samantha wondered what they would do if Wormley followed them into the woods. She hoped he would be satisfied with just scaring James, and that he would continue his hunt.

She smiled to herself realizing that Wormley would have to. He couldn't ride into the forest. The trees were too thick for a man to remain in the saddle. He would have to turn back, let his hounds flush the fox, and hunt in the open fields.

When they reached the dogwood tree, they stopped. Silence fell over the forest. The dogs yelped, heading north on the fox's trail.

"He . . . he . . . he shot at me," James choked out as his breath returned. "Why?"

"Maybe he thought you were the fox?" she joked, tugging on his red hair.

James lifted his head and looked at his sister. Her unruly hair spread from beneath her hat. She stuffed it back, picked up his hat, and rammed it on his head.

"If you kept your hat on, maybe you wouldn't have this trouble." It was a silly thing to say, but what else could she say to ease his fear?

Wormley was as mean as a water moccasin. They both knew to stay clear of him. Samantha hoped he wouldn't cause Papa trouble over this.

She was wrong.

As they came around the corner of their tobacco shed, Samantha saw Papa facing Wormley and his hunting friends. Each wore a red cloth badge on his sleeve. Wormley's tight face belied his anger. Samantha thrust the turkey at James.

"You keep your young ones off my land, Byrd," Wormley ordered, "or I might mistake one of yer red-headed litter for fox."

"You raise one hand against any of my children and you'll answer to me for it," Papa said sternly.

Wormley sniffed the air like he smelled pig manure. "Just because you folks have been in Virginia since the first days of Jamestown doesn't give you any special rights," Wormley snarled. "You can't just trample a man's tobacco field and ruin his hunt."

"Papa," Samantha cut in. Papa hadn't seen her approach; his eyes had been fastened on Wormley's. "He's lying, Papa."

Wormley swung in his saddle, glaring at the intrusion.

"There's one of them now," he growled.

"Samantha, you keep out of this," Papa said.

"No," replied Samantha.

Papa turned his full attention on her. She melted under his gaze.

"You and James go into the house. You've caused enough trouble."

Papa's steely eyes cut off her protest.

Reluctantly Samantha went to the house. Mama stood on the porch.

Wormley continued his tirade. "Byrd, your daughter runs wild. You ought to put a skirt on her like any other female."

Papa's fists clenched and unclenched. He struggled to keep his temper under control. Samantha gripped the musket so hard it hurt. She knew how he felt. Folks round about said the Byrds' tempers were as fiery as their red hair. It was true, except for James. He was her twin in looks only. In everything else they were as different as tobacco and corn.

Papa let Wormley spout off until he ran down. The other hunters listened, nodding. The hounds lay in the dust, panting. Samantha thought about fetching water for them.

" . . . And if I ever catch a Byrd so much as looking at my land, I'll, I'll . . . "

Before Wormley could finish, Papa unclenched one hand, flattening it out so it was as wide as a skillet.

"I'll thank you to get off my property, Thomas Wormley," Papa said. "And your Tory friends as well."

Wormley locked his snake eyes with Papa's eyes for a long moment. Papa held his gaze. Finally, Wormley looked away. Snatching the reins, he turned his horse.

Faster than lightning, Papa smacked the horse's rump. Wormley, his musket waving, struggled to hold on as his horse galloped out of the yard. His companions wheeled and followed, grins creeping onto their faces. The hounds trailed behind.

Mama firmly pushed down Samantha's musket. Samantha blushed. She had not even realized she had raised it.

"Thou shall not kill," Mama stated.

Samantha trembled. In her anger she had raised her gun against someone.

Chapter 4

Samantha rose before dawn. She listed all that she needed to take to Williamsburg. In a burlap sack were two rabbits she had snared last evening. Plump oysters sloshed in a barrel in the bow of her skiff, the *Fish Hawk*. She would pull the crate of fresh crabs out of the tide water, along with a stringer of fish she had caught at sunset. A dozen turtles crawled in the box in the *Fish Hawk*'s stern.

Henry was gone. Samantha had offered to take him to Williamsburg, but he turned her down, saying he had someone to meet on the way. She marveled at his stamina. He came home well after she had turned in. Even her sister Martha's restless muttering in the bed they shared hadn't kept Samantha awake last night.

When the first cardinal called she was eager to be off to

Williamsburg. But now she had to wait for James to wash before Mama would serve breakfast.

Samantha walked up to the house. The smell of hot johnnycakes and maple syrup greeted her. She dipped a finger into the syrup and quickly licked it before Mama could catch her. Mama did, and she frowned at her youngest daughter.

"Is James ready?" Samantha asked, innocently.

"He's changing," Martha answered, sneering at her. "Samantha, you aren't going to Williamsburg looking like that, are you?" she asked.

"Have you ever sailed a skiff in a skirt?" Samantha retorted.

"Mama, make her dress like a lady. I'll die of embarrassment if any of my friends see her," Martha complained.

Samantha made a face at her 17-year-old sister. She would be glad when Martha finally married—if any man would have her.

"Samantha, Martha's right," Mama said. "Change into your dress when you to get to Sarah's house," Mama ordered.

"But, Mama," Samantha protested.

"Do as your mother says, Samantha," Papa said, coming in behind her. He smelled of horses and hay. "It is only for the day."

Samantha thought of the tight teal-colored dress hanging in her sister Sarah's house. The color reminded her of a male mallard's head, but the thought of wearing the breath-killing corset took away that pleasure. At least she could keep on her comfortable moccasins. They would be hidden under her long skirt.

"I'd sooner stand in the stocks than wear a dress all day."

"I'm sure that could be arranged," Mama said, bending over a pot of porridge bubbling in the fireplace.

Papa hid a smile behind his hand as he pretended to yawn.

It was useless to argue. If she persisted, she might not even be able to go to town. All of her hard work gathering oysters and crabs, trapping turtles, hunting game, would be wasted if she couldn't get to town. Her dream of putting silver pennies into Papa's hand to help buy land or to help send James to William and Mary would fizzle like rain-dampened gunpowder.

Samantha smiled to herself. *I'll wear the dress*, she thought, *and I'll be the best-behaved young woman in Williamsburg. That will shock them.*

James sat down at the long pine table. He had combed his hair and put on his best white linen shirt. He would ride to town with Mama, Martha, and Papa in the wagon pulled by Jasper, their plow horse. James would spend the day with his friend George Lee at William and Mary.

Martha chattered away about the friends she would meet, many of whom she hadn't seen since they last visited Williamsburg. As she ate, Samantha thought of what a pleasant day that had been: eating, laughing, talking at Sarah's home. Pleasant except for having to wear her dress. And for the men's talk of Lord Dunmore.

"Dunmore is nothing but a pirate," Sarah's husband

Lem had complained. "First, he steals our gunpowder, then he hides away on his ship on the York River and raids honest Virginia farmers. He threatened to bombard York. Now he's inciting slaves to join him in his pirating."

Papa had agreed, adding, "They pressed men and boys against their will to man their five ships."

"I heard tell of a lad not much older than James and Samantha who drowned trying to escape from the *Kingfisher*," Lem continued. "Something must be done to stop them. Are we Virginians going to do nothing while our cousins in Massachusetts shed their blood at Concord and Bunker Hill fighting against similar outrages?"

"But what can we do?" Mama had asked. "Lord Dunmore is still the Royal Governor of Virginia."

"We can declare Virginia's independency from England!" Papa exclaimed. "We'll choose our own governor. Someone like Patrick Henry!"

This talk about war with England bored Samantha. She didn't care who governed Virginia or any of the other 12 colonies. She wanted to be free to hunt, fish, and roam the woods and waters. Live and let live.

"I can join the militia," James chimed in.

"You are not old enough," Papa told him. "You have to wait until your 16th birthday."

Samantha knew that was not necessarily true. Her 15-year-old cousin Matthew marched with the militia whenever the call to arms came. *He'll certainly be in town today*, she thought. *Maybe he'll come back with us.*

Matthew liked nothing better than to be with

Samantha in her skiff, hunting, fishing, and trapping. However, his father, Papa's older brother, John, a wealthy Williamsburg merchant, usually needed Matthew's help at his store.

James dropped a spoon. The clatter startled Samantha out of her daydream.

"I'd better get started," she said. "I need to be in town early to make the best deals. And the tide is running my way."

"I wish you would let me carry some of your goods in my wagon," Papa offered.

Samantha shook her head. "You have enough in your wagon already, Papa."

"You're as stubborn as your Ma," Papa said, shaking his head.

Mama cleared her throat and looked at her husband. "Stubborn runs on both sides of the stream in this family," she remarked. Then she looked at Samantha. "I expect you in your dress," she said, arching her eyebrows.

Samantha stood and curtsied. "Yes, Mama," she said sweetly.

Mama shook her head as Samantha grabbed her musket. She was out the door before Mama could scold her. She ran down the hill to their dock. Red-winged blackbirds balanced on the tops of reeds, swaying in the morning breeze. Ripples ran up the creek on the incoming tide. With the current and the wind going her way, Samantha would be in Williamsburg before the sun reached the treetops.

She bent down to untie the rope to her skiff. There was no rope.

Her heart dropped. There was no skiff!

The *Fish Hawk* was gone!

Chapter 5

Samantha anxiously searched the creek banks. No *Fish Hawk*. She had double hitched the painter rope last evening after fishing. If the rope had worked loose, the skiff would have drifted downstream on the outgoing tide last night. It could be anywhere now! Maybe even out onto the choppy waters of the James River.

"Where's my boat?" she shouted.

A heron, startled at her outburst, winged its way over the water. Blackbirds lifted off the reeds. Tears welled up in Samantha's eyes. She fought back the tears. The *Fish Hawk* wouldn't have gone far. The drag of her crab pot would slow the boat, maybe even anchor her. She might even be grounded on a mud bank.

Papa's old dugout canoe lay upside down on the bank under the wharf. Carefully setting her rifle on the dock,

Samantha climbed down to the canoe. She dragged it to the water, stepping in over the tops of her leather moccasins. She didn't care. She had to find the *Fish Hawk*.

Water seeped into the canoe through a crack running from bow to stern. She snatched a long stick, climbed into the canoe, and poled away from the shore. If the canoe sank, she would swim after her boat.

The incoming tide, her ally going upriver, was her enemy now, fighting her, pushing her opposite the way she wanted to go. Gritting her teeth, she jammed down the pole and strained against the stream. Slowly, she conquered the current and made headway.

She poled around one bend, then another. She struggled past a towering cedar, topped by an osprey's nest. Her eyes darted along the shore, hoping her own osprey, her *Fish Hawk*, had stopped drifting.

The crack of a gun rode the breeze from around the next point. Someone hunting.

She dug the pole in again and again. Her arms ached, the muscles protesting at her determination.

She rounded the point and saw the *Fish Hawk*.

A man scrambled up the shore. Samantha stared as he dashed into the dark forest. A bright red splotch of blood spread on his right shoulder.

"Sam!" a voice yelled.

She turned and looked back over her shoulder. Henry rammed a new ball down his musket. He had shot the man stealing her boat.

Samantha couldn't stop now. She poled across the

current and slid the canoe into the mud next to her skiff. She leaped from the dugout into her boat. A quick survey showed nothing damaged. Even her crab pot had been carefully pulled and stowed, the crabs crawling around in it looking for an escape route.

But who had taken her boat? And why?

Henry's voice came over the water. "How about a ride home?" he called.

"I'm coming," she hollered. She got out, shoved the skiff into deeper water, tied on the canoe, raised the sail, and within minutes had taken Henry aboard.

Chapter 6

"I winged him," Henry said as he settled into the *Fish Hawk*.

Samantha poled the boat into the channel and cleated the sail. The breeze, along with the tide, pushed them upstream.

"Thank goodness you did, or he would have gotten away with my boat. Who was he?" Samantha asked. "Why was he stealing my boat?"

"I'm not sure," Henry answered. "But there was something familiar about him." Henry swatted a mosquito as it settled on his arm. "I reckon I don't know why he was stealing your boat. Maybe he meant to sell your stuff down Newport way."

"Your shot should teach him to keep his thieving hands off my boat," Samantha stated.

"I've seen him somewhere," Henry puzzled. "Just can't recall when or where."

Samantha had the same feeling that she had seen the man before but couldn't recognize him. He wasn't from any nearby farm or plantation. Strangers were rare in these parts, but with the unrest spreading . . .

Her thoughts were cut short as Henry suddenly shouted, "I know where I saw him. He was riding with Wormley on his hunt!"

"But you weren't around during the hunt," Samantha said.

Henry smiled. "I was keeping an eye on James until you got him under your wing again. I almost shot Wormley myself when he shot at James."

"Why didn't you?" Samantha asked, her anger flaring.

"You don't think Wormley really tried to hit James, do you?"

Samantha thought for moment. "No, but he came dangerously close."

"He wanted to scare James and scare Papa in the process."

"Papa doesn't scare."

"But Wormley knows Papa wants some of his land, and he doesn't plan to sell any to Papa. When Wormley leaves for England, it won't make any difference." Henry said that last part as if he knew a secret.

"Why are you so sure he'll leave?" Samantha asked.

Henry grinned. "The Sons of Liberty have ways of persuading him," Henry said mysteriously.

Samantha wondered what they were, but a gust of wind brought all of her attention to bear on keeping the *Fish Hawk* in the channel. They rounded the last bend before their wharf.

"Mind if I join you?" Henry asked. "I was meaning to go to Williamsburg later today."

"I'd love it," Samantha exclaimed, eager for more of Henry's company. "I need to stop, leave Papa's canoe, and fetch my musket."

Samantha and Henry rode the wind and the tide towards Williamsburg. They watched the wilderness around them. Deer drank at the creek's edge, their footprints crisscrossing the mud. A muskrat was building a lodge. Samantha planned to trap it later in the fall when its pelt was thick.

A blue heron cried, "Kraannkk. Kraannkk," and flew downstream. Usually Samantha enjoyed the flight of the herons. Today, however, her thoughts returned to the strange man stealing her boat. "Henry, do you think Wormley was trying to get Papa angry by having his friend steal my boat?"

"Don't rightly know. Makes sense to me. He'd like nothing better than to get Papa riled so he would have an excuse for doing him some more harm."

"Why does Wormley hate Papa so much?"

"Has something to do with the French and Indian War. Papa and Wormley served in the same brigade. They were close friends then. But something happened that turned them into enemies."

"It's not Papa wanting independency and Wormley being a Tory?" Samantha asked. "After all, that war ended in 1763, when I was just a year old."

"It goes deeper than Papa wanting the British out of Virginia," Henry explained. "It has something to do with Papa's leg wound."

Samantha meant to ask Papa about this when they met in Williamsburg.

Henry turned his gaze upon Samantha. "Sam, it would be best if you didn't say anything to Papa about the boat being stolen and me shooting that stranger."

"But . . . " Samantha protested.

Henry continued. "You can tell him later, after I've had time to check something. Promise me, Sam."

Samantha hesitated, then said, "I promise. It's the Sons of Liberty, isn't it?"

Henry nodded.

Samantha adjusted the sheet, pretending to trim the full sail even though it didn't need it.

"Listen," Henry said, pointing upstream.

Samantha cocked an ear. At first she did not hear a sound. Gradually, she heard faint cries punctuated with the bleating of sheep. They were near Williamsburg, and the fair was well under way. They rounded two more bends. Samantha saw the red brick buildings of the College of William and Mary.

"I'll tie up at Uncle John's pier," Samantha said, steering the *Fish Hawk* with one hand while she released the sheet, spilling the air from the sail. The boat glided the last few feet to the dock, bumping it gently. Henry leaped out, the painter in his hand. He quickly tied off the boat. With Henry's help, Samantha unloaded the *Fish Hawk* in less than five minutes.

"Hey, Sam," someone called. Samantha looked up and saw her cousin Matthew coming her way. "I'll help you with those things."

"I'll see you at home this evening, Sam," Henry said.

Henry turned, smacked Matthew on the back, headed up the dirt path into town, and disappeared into the crowd.

Matthew said, "Anything here for Pa?"

Samantha's mouth dropped open like a gasping fish.

Thomas Wormley melted into the crowd behind Henry.

Chapter 7

"Matthew, stay here and watch my things," Samantha ordered. "I'll be right back." Samantha was gone before he could protest. She ran up the bank and stood on her tiptoes to try to see Henry. Too many people blocked her view. She pushed past housewives and cooks doing their day's shopping. Farmers stood by baskets of eggs, tubs of butter and cheese, and live chickens. Vendors called out their wares. One sold fresh fish. Another hawked oysters and crabs. Some had freshly slaughtered or live cattle for sale. On fair day, one could buy or trade everything from apples to bullet lead.

Children dashed here and there, chasing dogs or being chased. Pigs in makeshift pens grunted. Sheep bleated noisily. There were puppet shows and cockfights. On the green, someone was tuning a fiddle.

After the quiet on the creek, the noise of the fair overwhelmed Samantha. She darted hither and yon looking for Henry's brown weather-beaten hat. She also kept her eyes peeled for Thomas Wormley.

After half an hour of searching she gave up. As she walked back she hoped Matthew had stayed with her things. He had. Much to her pleasure he had even carried the perishable items up the bank. He stopped when he saw Samantha coming.

"Sam, where in the world did you rush off to?" he asked. "You ran off like you'd seen a ghost."

Samantha hesitated, not sure just how much to tell Matthew. Besides Henry and James, he was the closest person she had to another brother. "Oh, we had some trouble with Thomas Wormley yesterday. Then today someone stole *Fish Hawk*. I saw Wormley trailing Henry, but I could not catch either one."

"Let's shift this stuff," said Matthew. "I'll help you set up a place outside Father's store like you usually do. If you can sell most of this by noon, we can spend the afternoon enjoying the fair."

"Thank you, Matthew," Samantha said, knowing full well that Henry and Wormley might not be in Williamsburg by then. They could be in a tavern discussing trade or arguing. As a girl she could not enter a tavern to find them.

If only she were a boy.

Together Samantha and Matthew lugged the turtles, crabs, oysters, and other things she had to sell. Matthew had placed a long board across two barrels outside his father's store.

"Can you sell while I change my clothes?" Samantha asked Matthew. "Mama will have a fit if she sees me in these clothes. She, Papa, Martha, and James should be here soon. I won't be long." Samantha picked half a dozen of her best crabs out of the pot and dropped them in a burlap sack.

"I'd be glad to, Sam," Matthew said. "Father doesn't need me today. Says I'll just get underfoot."

"Thank you," Samantha called over her shoulder as she ran down a side street and up an alley to her sister Sarah's home.

Samantha stood on the steps for a moment, catching her breath. She pushed thoughts of Wormley and Henry out of her head. She took a deep breath and lifted the latch. She had to leave the world of the woods behind and become a proper young woman. It was easy for Samantha to switch roles. It didn't last long, and she made a game of it. But oh, that corset would be the death of her. Maybe she could get away without wearing it, she thought, or at least persuade Sarah not to tie it too tight.

The smell of bread hot from the oven greeted Samantha as she opened the door. She stood her musket in the corner as her niece and nephew tumbled around her like puppies.

"You smell all smoky," said Luke, the older child.

"That's from a campfire in the woods to scare off the bears," she growled at him.

"You don't look like a girl," Luke's sister Mary said.

"That's because I'm both a boy and a girl," she said. She bowed like a boy, whisked off her hat, curtsied like a lady, and showered her red hair over her niece.

Mary giggled and ran for her mama's skirts.

Sarah laughed at her youngest sister and hugged her. She held her at arm's length and looked Samantha in the eyes. "Sam, you are changing, that's for sure. You won't be able to keep dressing like a boy much longer."

"We'll see," Samantha said, handing Sarah the sack of wriggling crabs.

The little ones gathered around, asking her questions and waiting for a treat. She reached into the leather pouch hanging from her waist. Each time she visited, Samantha brought any unusual things that she had collected in the woods or on the beach: heron feathers, shiny shells, driftwood shaped like ducks. This time she had four smooth, round quartz pebbles, two for each child. She poured them onto the table.

The pebbles disappeared into eager hands. Mary and Luke scattered like hummingbirds, finding quiet spots to examine their treasure.

"I ironed your dress yesterday," Sarah told Samantha. "It is hanging in the wardrobe. Go change. I'll be in in a moment to help with the corset."

"Do I have to wear the corset?" Samantha asked. "I hate it."

"I know, but Mama will scold both of us if you don't."

Samantha went upstairs into her sister's bedroom and

pulled the dress, two petticoats, and the corset out of the wardrobe. She spread them on the bed. Then she put a petticoat back, deciding that one was torture enough.

She undressed slowly from her Sam clothes and put on her Samantha ones.

Sarah came in as she slipped on the corset.

"Don't tie it too tight," Samantha begged. "I can't breathe with this thing on."

"But you won't have a fashionable figure if I don't," Sarah teased.

"Hang fashion!" Samantha argued. She took a deep, deep breath, filling her lungs and pushing against the corset as Sarah tightened it. When she let out her breath, the corset wasn't as tight as it should be.

As Samantha slipped on her dress, Sarah gathered her Sam clothes and said, "I have hot water boiling. I'll wash these while you sell your goods. We can all be together for dinner."

"Thank you, Sarah," Samantha said, reluctant to see her clothes go, but knowing they would be ever so much cleaner when she put them back on.

Luke and Mary stood opened-mouthed when Samantha came downstairs. Even though they had seen her change before, it always amazed them each time she did. Tucking her hair under a white linen cap, Samantha wiggled to get more comfortable in her corset. Then she walked back to Uncle John's store.

Matthew had sold her crabs. Half of the oysters remained. Her uncle's customers always seemed pleased with the quality of Samantha's foodstuffs.

Matthew jingled a handful of coins. "Business has been brisk," he said, handing her the coins. She placed them in her leather pouch before helping a waiting customer. It was Mistress Craig, whose husband was a silversmith and owner of the Golden Ball jewelry shop.

"Good morning, Mistress Craig," Samantha said.

"Hello, Samantha," she said. "How fresh are your oysters?"

"Gathered them myself just yesterday afternoon," she answered. "I saved the best for you."

Mistress Craig frowned and said, "I'm not sure why your mother allows it, but you do fetch the finest oysters this side of the Chesapeake. Mister Craig is always asking for your oysters. Prefers them to all others."

"It's all in knowing where to find their beds," Samantha explained.

"I'll take three dozen. Being as it is fair day, Mister Craig will want them at day's end."

Samantha thanked Mistress Craig and helped another customer. Whenever she had a chance, she scanned the crowd for Henry. She had to warn him. Henry was perfectly capable of defending himself, but still . . .

The sun hung overhead when they had sold the last of the crabs, fish, oysters, and turtles. The leather pouch thumped against Samantha's thigh. She would spend some of her money at the fair, but the rest would go to Papa.

Matthew wiped his forehead and sat on her crab crate. Samantha started to wipe her hands on her breeches, then remembered she was wearing a dress. She dumped the saltwater from her oyster barrel, then wiped her hands on a rag.

"I'll take these to the *Fish Hawk*," she told Matthew. "Then I'll see Uncle John. Treat you to the puppet show when I'm finished," she said.

The *Fish Hawk* was just as she had left it. She carefully placed the barrel and the pot into the boat. She checked to see if the painter was properly tied before returning to her uncle's shop.

Even though it was early September it felt good to be in the dark shop and out of the sun's glare. Uncle John stood behind his long counter. His shelves were almost bare today. Last Christmas they had been full, but not overflowing like they had been before the trouble with England began. But because so many Virginians had stopped buying or using British products, Uncle John had little call for such goods. Even if he had wanted things like tea, gunpowder, lead, English cloth, lace, pewter buttons, plates, and china, they were not available for sale because trade with the mother country had almost stopped.

Why can't the Americans and English get along? Samantha wondered again. *Then things would stay the same.* She ran her hands down the apron of her dress. The homemade linsey-woolsey apron was rough . . . *but at least it was made here at home*, she thought. *I am beginning to sound like a Virginia Patriot.*

Matthew followed her inside.

"Why, Miss Samantha Byrd!" exclaimed Uncle John. "Don't you look absolutely ravishing today!" he teased.

35

Samantha blushed. *Thank goodness it is so dark in here,* she thought, *or he would be teasing me about blushing too.*

"What are you needing?" he asked.

"Gunpowder and lead. I'm running low of both."

"Everyone is," Uncle John said. "The militia needs every ounce I can smuggle in. Since Dunmore raided the powder magazine, we've treasured every barrel. But I saved some, knowing you'd be here for the fair."

"Thank you," Samantha replied, placing two small silver coins on the counter. Then she turned around and said, "Come on, Matthew. Let's see the fair. What do you want to do first?" She was anxious to be back outside and looking for Henry.

"Let's look and then decide," said Matthew.

Samantha blinked as they returned to the bright sunlight. She wished she had her hat to shade her face. They joined the crowd strolling down toward Market Square where the fair was.

At one stall Samantha treated Matthew to bread. At another she bought cheese and cider. Then they watched a puppet show about a Virginian besting a British soldier in a shooting contest.

Suddenly they heard someone shout, "You should go back to England where you belong! If you like tobacco so much, here's some you can have."

A man no taller than Samantha took a large plug of wet tobacco out of his mouth and hurled it. Samantha didn't see who it hit, but she knew why the crowd had gathered. Some poor soul was in the stocks.

Samantha and Matthew elbowed their way through the crowd to get a better view. Standing on her tiptoes Samantha saw a man, his arms dangling through the stocks, his bent head dripping with gobs of tobacco.

"Who is it?" she asked.

"That English-loving Alfred Whitesides," someone said.

"What did he do?"

"Traded two cows to Dunmore's men."

Matthew spoke up. "He deserves this and worse." He threw a stone at the man. Samantha picked up a rock too, but decided it wouldn't be ladylike to throw it, so she dropped it.

"Should have been tarred and feathered," the man said.

Matthew agreed. Samantha was not so sure.

When they worked their way to the edge of the crowd, she asked Matthew, "Why should he be punished for trading with Dunmore's men? Isn't Dunmore still the Royal Governor?"

"In the eyes of King George, yes, but not in the eyes of Virginians. Dunmore's our enemy now."

Samantha understood why Papa was angry with King George for not honoring the Crown's commitment to the men who had fought the French and Indians. Papa had been promised 200 acres of prime land west of the Blue Ridge for his army service, especially since he had been wounded and would carry his limp to his grave. Lord Dunmore had claimed 20,000 acres for himself and his family, but none was forthcoming for the soldiers.

Matthew explained. "First, he stole gunpowder from the magazine. Then he fled like a thief in the night. Now he commands a fleet of five ships. He has called all patriotic Virginians rebels and promises to hang them. That means my father, your father, and Henry. He plans to put Virginia under his dung-covered heel."

Samantha looked at her cousin. Normally quiet Matthew, content to hunt and fish with her without hardly saying a word, had just spoken a waterfall of words. He sounded just like Papa and the rest of the men who condemned Dunmore.

Samantha wiggled in her corset, trying to get more comfortable.

"Is this why you joined the militia and gave up sailing on your father's ship?"

"Yes," Matthew answered. "Henry and dozens of others have joined. You'll see how many when we march this afternoon." He paused. "You will stay, won't you?"

Samantha agreed and they continued their tour of the fair.

Across the open square they heard delighted screaming and shouting. "Let's see what that is about," Samantha suggested. "Race you!" she said, and lifting her skirt, took off running. Matthew, caught off guard, couldn't catch her. Even in a fair race he couldn't catch Samantha.

When he stood panting beside her, Samantha said, "They are playing Soap'd Pig. It costs a halfpenny to play. Whoever catches the pig gets to keep it. I'll treat you."

Two men wrestled with the squealing pig. One man

held its legs. Another smeared lye soap on the wiggling animal. A third held out his hat for the pennies being dropped in it by the players.

Samantha tugged Matthew in her wake. She untied her leather pouch, pulled out a penny, and dropped it into the hat.

"What about your dress?" Matthew asked.

Samantha looked at her clothes. She had forgotten she had on her one and only dress. Before she could change her mind, the man released the pig.

The pig ran in a circle, then broke through the crowd. People leaped out of its way as a dozen boys dashed after it. One grabbed the pig's hind legs. It slipped right out of his hands. Another grabbed the pig's back. His hands slipped off too.

With a whoop, Samantha joined the chase. She wasn't going to lose her halfpenny.

The pig turned this way and that, dodging its pursuers. He came toward Samantha. She grabbed at him but missed. Matthew lunged at the pig as it came his way. He gripped a leg, but the pig wiggled free. Yelling, the others circled the pig.

Samantha had a mud puddle to her right. The pig ran in her direction. She spread her legs and stood firmly in its path. The pig had to swerve left to escape. But the pig had other plans. It ran directly at Samantha and veered to the right, straight into the mud puddle. Without hesitating, Samantha jumped to block it. Her feet flew out from beneath her just as the pig hit the mud. Samantha landed flat on her back. The squealing pig slipped and slid right into her arms. She hugged it with all her might.

The crowd roared in laughter as Samantha wrestled the pig into submission.

Above the noise, Samantha heard Martha cry, "Oh, Mama! Look what Samantha has done now. I'm mortified."

Samantha looked over the pig's back, directly into Mama's eyes.

Chapter 8

Papa stood behind Mama, shaking with laughter. Mama shook her head and laughed too. Martha glared at Samantha.

Breathless, Matthew helped Samantha to her feet and took the pig from her arms. He handed the pig to a man who placed it in a nearby pen.

Mud dripped from Samantha's arms. Her dress was mud-covered. Her cap was off, and her hair flew in every direction.

Papa and Mama walked over as Martha stormed off to Sarah's house.

"Reckon that pig will fatten up some more by winter," Papa said, still holding his sides. "You are a sight, child."

"We can dress you up," Mama said, "but we sure can't make a lady out of you. Come on, let's get you changed into your old clothes before anything else happens."

Samantha's old clothes (as Mama called them) were clean but still damp from the washing Sarah had given them. Samantha felt relieved to be shed of the dress and corset.

Mama told her, "You will take your dress home, young lady, and wash it there. Sarah has more than enough work without you adding to her load."

"Yes, Mama," Samantha said meekly.

"And the corset too."

"Yes, Mama." Samantha, feeling ever so much better dressed in her regular clothes, wasn't about to argue.

Papa asked, "Has anyone seen Henry? We were to meet Uncle John to discuss business."

Mama arched her eyebrows. "What business?"

"I have five hogsheads of tobacco from last year's crop that I must sell by September 10. That's the last day we may ship to England. After that, all 13 colonies will stop trading with Great Britain. I want John to ship it on his trading vessel, the *Cardinal*."

Samantha looked puzzled. "I thought he stopped trading with England," she said.

"He will after this," said Papa. "Then he will trade only with the Dutch and the Spanish in the Indies. He'll trade pine boards, ham, corn, and wheat."

"And of course, tobacco," Mama said.

"What will he bring to Virginia?" Sarah asked. "I haven't seen a single bolt of silk in a year." She pretended to pout.

Papa scratched his head and looked away. "Don't rightly know," he said evasively.

The conversation was too complicated for Samantha, so she helped Sarah put food on the table. Dinner at Sarah's was always a feast. Today there was venison stew, crab cakes, boiled crabs, succotash, cornbread, ham, cheese, and apple pie.

Samantha noticed that everything they ate had been grown or raised or caught in Virginia. She wanted a hot cup of proper tea, but since 1774 only Tories drank English tea. That is, if they could get it. Samantha missed English tea. The homemade Liberty Tea that they drank tasted like dirty dishwater. *If only we could get along*, she thought.

After dinner, Samantha bundled her soggy clothes, took her musket, and said goodbye to her sister and her family. "I'll meet you at the farm," she said to Mama and Papa. "I want to ride the outgoing tide home after the militia marches. I promised Matthew I'd watch."

Papa said, "Wait, Samantha. I'll walk with you. I have to fetch James at the college. Henry will be with the militia."

Samantha and Papa walked to Market Square. The open green field was filled with men carrying muskets, rifles, and small arms. Most wore dark-stained hunting shirts with leather fringe dangling from the sleeves. The hunting shirts, like Henry's, were the closest things the Virginians had to a uniform.

Samantha and Papa joined the crowd to watch the

militia drill. A drum rattled. A fifer played the popular new tune "Yankee Doodle." The crowd joined in. Samantha smiled as Papa added his deep bass voice to the song. She liked the music but did not join in. To her it was one more thing keeping Americans and English apart.

The militiamen fell in behind the fifer and marched across the green. A tall man, skinny as a loblolly pine, gave orders. As he shouted, the men turned one way, then another. Some stumbled trying to keep up with their companions. Others turned right when the rest turned left. Henry and Matthew knew what they were doing.

Papa sighed. "With a militia like this, how will we fight England's regular soldiers? When I was in the army, we could turn on a speck of dust. No man missed a step. We carried our rifles properly, not like a bunch of woodcutters."

Samantha remembered that she wanted to ask Papa about Thomas Wormley. Papa rarely talked about the French and Indian War. When he returned from the fighting, he swore never to raise a gun against another man again except in self-defense. Samantha could not even imagine what it must feel like to sight a person along the long barrel of a gun, and then pull the trigger.

Papa never talked about Wormley's role in the war, but Samantha's curiosity overwhelmed her. She had to know, especially now as there was more trouble with Mr. Wormley.

"Papa, what is between you and Mr. Wormley?"

Papa's eyes had that faraway look that he got when he

wanted to avoid discussing something. The same faraway look Henry got when he talked about going over the Blue Ridge Mountains to Kentucky.

Papa looked at his daughter, her bundle of clothes and musket in her hands, and said, "Let's sit by Uncle John's store. You are old enough to know the reason for the bad blood between us."

Samantha stood her musket against the store wall and set her wet bundle on the end of a wooden bench.

Papa took a deep breath and began, "During the French and Indian War, Thomas Wormley and I served together. We weren't regular soldiers, but militia. Like so many farmers, shopkeepers, and lawyers were. Wormley was chosen captain of our unit because he owned the largest plantation. We were friends still. Not enemies. Yet."

"What happened?" Samantha asked, squeezing Papa's hand.

"We were in the Ohio Valley when the Shawnees and French ambushed us. I was shot in the leg and went down. Wormley saw me lying there, but the fighting was thick and furious. We were almost surrounded. Still, the men fought bravely on. That is, everyone but Wormley. Thinking no one had seen him, he ducked into the forest out of the battle. When we had driven the Frenchies and Shawnees away, he came crawling back like the coward he is. He knew from the look in my eyes that I had witnessed his cowardliness. From that day to this, he has hated me."

Papa stretched his injured leg and stood. He glanced at the sun dipping in the west. "You'd best be going if you want to catch the tide. Slack water has passed. I'll fetch Mama, Martha, and James home."

He looked at his daughter. "Samantha," he said. "What I told is just within our family. No sense spreading more ill will."

Samantha's thoughts were jumbled. She needed time to sort her feelings. She nodded and said, "Thank you, Papa, for telling me. See to my pig, please."

"I will. Fresh bacon will taste wonderful come the first hard freeze."

The crowd thinned. The militia stopped drilling, and the men scattered to the taverns. Most folks living in Williamsburg retired for the evening. Those in for the fair from their farms and plantations had packed their wagons and were rolling out of town. Trails of dust followed them.

Samantha hurried. Night was not far off.

As she untied the *Fish Hawk*, Matthew called, "Sam, may I come with you? Papa says I can visit for a few days, now that the fair is over and the militia has practiced."

Samantha smiled. "Of course, you can," she said. "We will be pleased to have you."

"Can we hunt? Papa gave me powder and lead for five shots."

"I know where deer come to the river to drink," she said. "We can go at sunset tomorrow." Samantha paused. "Did you talk with Henry?"

"Yes," Matthew answered. "He came to the store to speak with Papa while you were gone. He said to tell your parents he would be home later tonight. He and the Sons of Liberty have business this evening."

Samantha concentrated on getting the *Fish Hawk* moving downstream in the current. The *Fish Hawk* glided on the ebbing tide. The falling evening breeze filled the sail just enough to move them gently along. As they drifted, Samantha and Matthew enjoyed the fiery setting sun, the bats darting after insects, and the frogs jumping. A woodpecker pecked for insects in an old pine. Rat-a-tat-tat.

"James was wondering if woodpeckers ever get headaches," Samantha said.

She and Matthew laughed.

"Only James would wonder that," Matthew said.

Samantha showed Matthew where the deer drank. She also pointed out the lodge of the muskrat that she planned to trap this winter. She and Matthew plotted the expeditions they would make while Matthew was visiting. They would hunt. Fish down on the James River. Maybe even sail partway to Norfolk if the winds were right.

Samantha saw the smoke first. "Look, Matthew!" She pointed over the forest.

"Someone's burning trees to clear a new tobacco field," Matthew suggested.

Samantha stared at the rising smoke. She took an oar and handed it to Matthew. "Paddle," she ordered. "That fire is coming from our farm!"

Samantha dug her oar into the water. Whirls followed each dip as they paddled as hard as they could. Samantha kept her eye on the smoke. They rounded one bend, then another, and finally a third before the Byrd farm came into view.

"Our tobacco shed is on fire!" Samantha shouted.

Chapter 9

Pungent, black smoke swirled from the flames devouring the tobacco shed. The roof had collapsed. One wall remained. As they stared, yellow flames licked it. There was nothing they could do but watch the shed burn.

Papa's hopes for buying more land died with the rising smoke. This was his last tobacco crop unless he got more land. Growing tobacco was so hard on the soil that new land was constantly needed to grow it. His land was used up, worn out. He had already switched to corn to raise food for Virginian soldiers. Now he would have no choice but to raise wheat too. The best money, however, lay in tobacco. Money that could send James to William and Mary. Money to help Henry buy land west of the Blue Ridge. If only he had received the land promised him for his war services. Then everything would be fine.

If only.

While Samantha gazed at the blaze, Matthew bent down and picked up a piece of crimson cloth.

"What is it?" Samantha asked as she took it from Matthew.

"A royalist badge," Matthew explained. "Just as we Patriots wear hunting shirts, Tories wear these red cloth badges."

"Whoever set the fire must have dropped it!" she exclaimed. "Wormley and his friends."

"Wait until your father sees this," Matthew said. "He will be madder than a cornered sheep!"

Just then, the wagon rolled into the farmyard. "Giddyap, you old nag!" Papa shouted at Jasper. Papa leaped out before the wagon stopped. "What in thundering tarnation happened?" he bellowed.

Samantha held out the red badge.

Papa threw it down. He ground it into the dirt with the heel of his boot. "Wormley is going to pay this time," he growled. "The Sons of Liberty will see to it."

"How do you know it was Wormley?" Mama asked.

"Has to be," Papa said. "Nobody else is mean enough to burn a man's tobacco."

"He is meaner than a nest of disturbed water moccasins," James chimed in.

Martha came up, crying. "What are we going to do?" she sniffed. "There won't be money for sugar this winter. Or new lace. Or . . . "

Samantha sneered at her sister. *She is the most selfish creature in Virginia*, she thought. She didn't dare say it out loud for fear of Mama's reaction.

Papa took one last look at his burning shed and turned on his heels. "Let's unload the wagon before it is too dark," he said.

Samantha took charge of her pig. It had trotted home behind the wagon and lay exhausted in the dust. She brought water in a pan. Then she led the pig to the pen beside the barn. The pig wallowed in the dirt and settled in a corner.

"I'll bring you slops later," Samantha promised.

James unhitched Jasper, let him drink his fill at the water trough, and fed him hay and oats.

Mama and Martha went to prepare supper.

After feeding her pig, Samantha carried in an armload of firewood. She stirred the coals and added pine splinters for kindling. As the flames grew, she put in bigger pieces. She went to the well, filled a kettle with water, and hung it over the fire to heat.

Papa took his rifle from its pegs over the door. He oiled the long barrel and replaced the flint. He rattled his powder horn to check his powder and put new lead bullets into his pouch.

Mama watched him without saying a word. But when he stood up to leave, she blocked the doorway. "William Byrd, don't you even think about going to Wormley's plantation alone. He's bound to have friends waiting for you to rush in like a wild boar. That's just what he wants you to do, the coward that he is." Mama knew all about Wormley's cowardice.

"I'll go," Matthew volunteered. "Then Uncle William won't be alone."

"I'll go too," Samantha said.

"Me too," James added.

Mama crossed her arms. "Not one of you is going to cross this sill unless you want to tangle with me."

Papa stared at Mama, shrugged his shoulders, and put the rifle back on its pegs. Samantha frowned. Why had Papa backed down?

"You are right, dear," he said. "We can deal with this in the morning. Henry will be here then."

"You and Henry can go. I can't stop you. You are grown men." Mama turned to look at Samantha, Matthew, and James. "But you three, get any notion of going right out of your heads this very second."

"Yes," they chorused.

Samantha caught Matthew's eye. He was thinking the same thing. They would find a way to join the men in the morning.

"Your water is boiling over," Martha said sweetly to Samantha.

Samantha dashed to the fire and swung off the pot. She dipped out four bucketfuls and sloshed them into the wooden washtub that Papa had made from an old tobacco hogshead. Mama handed her a bar of lye soap. Samantha cleaned her muddy dress and corset. When she finished, her fingers were wrinkled, and she hated the dress more than ever. She hung it by the fire to dry overnight.

James and Matthew had already climbed up to the loft.

She heard them settling down on their corn husk mattresses.

Martha was in bed when Samantha entered the small room they shared. Samantha set down her candle and looked back. Papa was staring out the window, watching the last of the shed burn. A shower of sparks shot into the sky. He stood clenching and unclenching his fists. Samantha wondered what he was thinking. He stayed that way even after she blew out the candle.

Samantha quickly undressed and climbed into bed. She pushed the blanket to the side. It was too hot to sleep under it tonight. She closed her eyes. The day had been long, and she slipped quickly to sleep.

Chapter 10

Papa's and Henry's voices woke her.

"The farm smells like every pipe at Raleigh's Tavern being smoked at once," Henry said.

"Wormley burnt our tobacco shed," Papa told him.

"What!" Henry exclaimed.

Mama said, "Hush! You'll wake the children."

Papa led Henry outside. Samantha heard their footsteps heading toward the shed. Ever so slowly, she felt along the cabin wall until her fingers touched a piece of cloth. She pulled on the cloth, revealing a narrow gap in the wall.

Samantha sniffed and rolled over as if she were trying to get more comfortable. She didn't dare wake Martha. A glimmer of moonlight shone through the hole. Not even Mama knew the hole was there. When Samantha was little, she used to look through it and watch chickens peck or puppies roughhouse. Now Samantha used the hole to check the daylight when she went early-morning hunting. She couldn't see Papa and Henry, but she could hear them.

"What are we going to do?" Henry asked.

"I want you to ride over to Daniel Walker's. He and his boys are the nearest members of the Sons of Liberty. Ride with them to the crossroads. I'll meet you there. We'll ride on to Wormley's together."

"Are you expecting trouble, Papa?" Henry asked.

"I'm not sure if Wormley's friends are still there. The more of us, the better chance we have of catching him. Tell Daniel to bring a pillow."

Why would he need to bring a pillow? Samantha wondered.

"I'll bring the tar," Papa said.

Samantha drew in her breath. They were going to tar and feather Wormley. This she had to see!

She slipped quietly out of bed and dressed quickly. She listened to Mama's gentle snoring and stole past her to the loft ladder. She climbed up to wake Matthew. He would never forgive her if she saw the tar and feathering without him.

The loft was as dark as the bottom of a well. Samantha stood still, and like a hunter on the trail of her quarry, she listened. She heard both boys breathing. Which one was Matthew?

She knelt down and put out her hand. She felt an arm. She shook it and whispered, "Matthew?"

"What do you want?" came a sleepy voice. It was

James!

"It's me, Sam," she said. "Don't make a sound or you will wake Mama."

She heard Henry gallop away.

"James, wake up Matthew. Something's going on."

James grunted and poked Matthew.

"What is it? It's too early to go hunting," Matthew said.

Samantha hissed, "Shh. Don't say another word. Just follow me."

"I'm coming too," James said.

"No, you are not," Samantha told him.

"Then I'll wake Mama and tell her you went somewhere in the middle of the night."

"Oh, all right," Samantha said. "But no whining."

"I don't whine," James retorted.

Samantha wasn't about to argue with him. She just climbed back down the ladder. The boys followed silently.

Samantha paused by the door to take her hat. The boys got theirs as well. Samantha lifted the latch, and the three stepped into the night. She glanced around to see if she could spot Papa, but he was still in the barn.

Samantha led them to the dock. They huddled in the shadows and watched Papa lead Jasper out of the barn. Papa gripped a wooden bucket. Awkwardly, he climbed onto Jasper. The old horse trotted down the trail.

When Papa was out of sight, Samantha signaled for Matthew and James to follow her. *Thank goodness for the moonlight*, she thought as they trailed behind Papa.

When they were out of earshot of the house, Samantha

stopped. "Papa and Henry and the Walkers are going to tar and feather Wormley," she said.

"What!" James exclaimed.

"Tar and feather him for burning our tobacco," she said. "Don't you want to watch?"

"I wouldn't miss it for all the tea in England!" Matthew said.

"Me neither," James said.

"Then we'll have to hurry. We're on foot and they're on horses," Samantha told them. Without wasting another second, the three ran down the road.

The moon hovered overhead. Samantha guessed it was well past three in the morning. Dawn was not far away. They would have to hurry if they were going to see Wormley get his due and be back in bed before Mama awoke.

If only we had horses, Samantha thought. *If only there was a shorter way to Wormley's place.*

Samantha stopped so suddenly that Matthew bumped into her, and James crashed into Matthew.

"What in tarnation?" Matthew asked.

"We're going to take a shortcut," she said. "Otherwise we'll never get there in time."

Samantha looked around to get her bearings. They were halfway to Wormley's. If they followed the edge of his tobacco fields, they'd come to his slave quarters. They could slip past them and get to the main house before the others arrived.

She explained her plan to James and Matthew. When

they reached the field, they ran along it until they were in sight of the slave quarters.

Near the slave cabins, they stopped and listened. Samantha did not hear anything alarming. She motioned the boys on. They slipped behind the last cabin. Wormley's house loomed on a hilltop. Trees surrounded it like guards on duty. There were plenty of hiding places. Samantha thought, *We'll watch, leave, and be back home before anyone knows we're missing.*

Crash!

James kicked over a wooden pail.

"Hoowwll! Hoowwll!" Wormley's pack of hounds chorused.

Chapter 11

"Run!" Samantha shouted, pushing Matthew and James.

The dogs barked fiercely. Samantha looked back. Candlelight flickered in the big house. A gun blast split the night. The dogs howled as if after a bear. Samantha turned and ran and did not look again.

Out of breath, the three stopped deep in the woods.

"How could you be so stupid?" Samantha snarled at James.

"I hope he doesn't loose the dogs," he whimpered.

They listened intently. The dogs quieted. Without a word, the threesome trudged through the woods until they reached the road.

After a while, they stopped, this time listening for horses. Papa and Henry would return this way.

"Come on," Samantha urged. "We have to get home before Papa."

"Ah, Sam," complained James. "I can't go any further."

"You'll wish you had when Papa cuts a new switch."

James took a huge breath and started running. Samantha and Matthew were close behind.

Soon they heard the steady pounding of horses' hooves. "Here comes Papa," Samantha whispered. "Quick. Hide!"

"Where?" cried James.

"Oh, just follow me," she said, exasperated. If only he could do something right.

Samantha glanced around for a suitable hiding place. A massive oak stood off the trail. She crashed through the underbrush with Matthew and James behind her.

The beat of the horses' hooves reminded Samantha of the drummers in the militia. Was it only yesterday? So much had happened so fast that she could not keep track. They ducked behind the tree, panting like overheated dogs. In the dim light, they saw Papa and Henry gallop towards them.

"Stay still," Samantha ordered. No one moved until Papa and Henry had ridden past. They left their hiding place after the horses had disappeared around the bend.

"I hope there wasn't poison ivy," James whispered. He scratched his arms.

"If there was, you deserve to itch," Samantha said. "After all, you woke the dogs."

She stalked toward the farm.

Now what are we going to do? Samantha worried. They couldn't sneak past Papa and Mama. As soon as she lifted the latch, they would know.

If only they had beaten Papa back.

She stopped where the forest met their fields. Inside the house, a light glowed. Samantha sighed. They were in for a switching. Samantha rubbed her backside. She could already feel the switch's sting.

The sweet smell of tobacco lingered. The moon hung in a tall pine. To the east, the sky was brightening from black to gray. A new day had begun.

"Let face the music," Samantha said.

Matthew agreed.

James held back. "Wait, Sam," he snapped.

Chapter 12

Samantha stopped in her tracks. "Now what?" she hissed.

"Let's take the *Fish Hawk*," said James. "We'll pretend we went fishing early. Then we'll have an excuse for being gone."

Samantha considered his suggestion. It might work, especially since they hadn't wakened Mama when they left.

Samantha patted James on the back. "Let's try," she said.

Accepting her leadership again, the boys followed Samantha to the dock. They climbed into the skiff. Matthew sat in the bow, ready to untie the Fish Hawk when Samantha gave the command. James sat in the middle, eager to do something else to help.

"Cast off," she whispered. Matthew untied the painter and the *Fish Hawk* drifted away. The flowing tide was carrying them towards Williamsburg.

Samantha let them drift while she made up her mind what to do. Would it make a difference if they rode the incoming tide towards Williamsburg or paddled downstream? Either way they could fish. But where would they have the best chance of catching something? Downstream, she figured. So downstream they would go.

Samantha waited until they drifted out of earshot of the house. Then she said, "The current is taking us toward Williamsburg. We'll have to paddle the opposite direction."

"Right," Matthew said, grasping the situation.

He picked up an oar, gave James the other one, and they both began paddling. They were an awkward team at first. Once they settled into a rhythm, though, the *Fish Hawk* fought the current and won. A light flickered in the window of the Byrd house. They slipped silently past it and were soon several bends down College Creek.

The sun, a red, hazy ball, rose as they reached the broad James River. Patches of mist hung over the creek. Herons probed the mud for breakfast. Along the shore, a startled doe and her fawn bounded away into the forest's protection. Overhead, a searching fish hawk soared.

The boys paddled. Samantha steered and checked the water for wind ripples. She was puzzled. By now, with the sun peeking through the trees, and the mist disappearing, a breeze should be picking up. She could tell by the boat's motion that James and Matthew were tiring. The tide should turn soon.

When the tide turned, the boys dropped their oars and

dozed with their heads on the thwarts. The September sun burned down. Samantha was glad that she had her hat. Matthew had his, but James was bareheaded. He had lost his hat while they fled from Wormley.

Beads of sweat dripped from James's forehead. Samantha took off her hat and gently placed it on his head. Her tanned skin could take more weather beating.

Samantha glanced at the sun. An unnatural haze shrouded it. The river lay as flat as a sizzling griddle, heat waves dancing. Not a hint of breeze rippled the water. The sail hung as limp as wet washing. Something was not right, but Samantha could not put her finger on it.

James awoke first, hungry and thirsty. Samantha gave him water from the flask that she kept onboard. He looked around. He squinted at the water. He glanced at the sun. Not a fish jumped. Not a bird flew.

Suddenly he sat up and focused his gaze to the west, where black clouds towered.

"Hurricane," he whispered.

Samantha followed his gaze, her ears not believing. She had seen the clouds. Now she saw distant waves being pushed by the wind.

"It can't be!" she exclaimed. Even as she spoke, the first wave rocked the *Fish Hawk*. Within seconds, the wind slammed into them.

"What in tarnation?" Matthew said, shaken from his sleep.

"Hurricane," James repeated.

Samantha gripped the tiller and pulled the sail sheet tight. The *Fish Hawk*, her sails filled to bursting, leaped like a frightened deer.

"We will run with the wind as long as we can," she
said, raising her voice above the rising wind. "Lash down
anything loose. Hang on!"

The wind increased its push until the *Fish Hawk* flew
like her namesake, her bow slicing the water. The waves
surged behind them. They had to keep ahead of the waves
or they would swamp.

Samantha could turn the boat into the waves, and they
could fight their way into the gale. But when they tacked,
the wind would flip them like a toy. Their only chance was
to run with the wind at their backs and hope that the sail
would not rip to shreds. She could lower the sail to save it,
but the monstrous waves would flood them from the
stern.

Running with the wind was their only chance.

Ahead, a peninsula jutted out into the river. Trees,
flailing helplessly, were plucked from the earth as the wind
increased. With both hands on the tiller, Samantha aimed
the *Fish Hawk* toward the thumb of land.

Craaack!

Sounding like a musket shot, the sail split from
bottom to top.

"Drop the sail!" Samantha screamed, the wind ripping
her words away. Matthew uncleeted the sheet. The sail,
flapping like a wounded goose, dropped. Matthew and
James desperately furled the sail. Matthew, who was 20
pounds heavier than James, wrapped his arms around the
sail and hugged it to the boom while James lashed it. Then
he and James frantically stuffed loose gear into Samantha's

crab pots and tied down anything else.

Without the sail, the *Fish Hawk* was at the mercy of the wind and waves. Samantha looked forward toward shore and then back at the waves rising behind them. The *Fish Hawk* was light, riding the waves like a cork in a washtub. Up, down, up, down.

Thunder split the air. Jagged spears of lightning forked overhead. Pellets of rain stung them like wasps. A waterfall burst upon them. No stinging, just a solid wall of water. Samantha shouted for them to bail, but the wind snatched away her words. She grabbed James and yanked him. "Bail!" she shouted in his ear, thrusting a pail into his hand.

James scooped and dumped water overboard. Matthew splashed water out with his hands. The *Fish Hawk* no longer floated lightly. The skiff was heavy with water, and each wave threatened to fill it.

Samantha searched through the downpour for the shore. Angry water raged below them, around them, and above them.

She fought with the tiller to keep the stern facing the oncoming waves. They had to hit shore soon. She hoped they would strike it before they sank.

A fistful of wind smashed the *Fish Hawk* and yanked the tiller from Samantha's hands. The *Fish Hawk* skittered sideways, broadside to the waves.

"Hang on!" Samantha screamed.

The *Fish Hawk* flipped.

Chapter 13

The *Fish Hawk* turned turtle. Her mast pointed to the river bottom, her keel to the black sky.

Samantha went under. She held her breath and struggled to rise to the surface. Kicking with all her strength, she finally broke free.

The *Fish Hawk* had drifted away from Samantha. Blinking water from her eyes, she saw James clutching the keel. Matthew, holding onto a side plank, stretched a hand to her. She grabbed it, and he pulled her in. He pushed her up onto the bottom of the boat until she gripped the keel. Then he climbed up after her.

Breathless, Samantha surveyed their situation. The *Fish Hawk* floated well upside down. *Where is land?* she worried. They couldn't hang on and ride the waves for long.

She peered through the storm. A bolt of lightning lit the sky. Less than 100 yards ahead, waves crashed onto a beach. Samantha punched Matthew and pointed to the beach. He shook his head as if he didn't understand. The next flash of lightning showed him what she meant. He yelled her message into James's ear.

In a few moments, Samantha felt the mast snap as it struck the bottom. The *Fish Hawk* grated against the sand and ground to a stop.

"Get James on shore," she yelled above the howl of the wind. "Then come back to help me."

Matthew grabbed James, plunged into the surf, and struggled out of reach of the water. He pushed James toward an uprooted tree. "Stay here!" he hollered before trudging against the wind back to Samantha.

Samantha reached under the *Fish Hawk*'s bow and gripped the painter. She handed it to Matthew and leaned towards him. "Wait for the next big wave," she called. "I'll get behind and push. You pull. We have to get her on the beach before she breaks apart."

The waves smacked Samantha as she struggled against them. Each wave shoved her against the stern, pinning her momentarily. She glanced behind her, watching for the big wave she prayed was coming. Seeing it, she screamed to Matthew.

The wave grew taller and taller until it broke with a rush of foam and roared up the shore. It lifted the *Fish Hawk* and carried her up the beach as Samantha and Matthew guided the boat. The next wave washed the stern as the skiff settled on the sand.

68

Samantha hugged Matthew in her relief. "Where is James?" she asked when she caught her breath.

Matthew pointed to a fallen pine, its roots ripped from the earth. The wind pushed them toward him. James had crawled under the massive trunk. They joined him. It wasn't much shelter, but it was all they had. The three huddled there as the hurricane raged around them.

What are we going to do now? Samantha worried. *We're stranded somewhere along the James River. We have no food. No water unless the flask is still lashed to the* Fish Hawk. *The mast is broken off, so we can't sail the* Fish Hawk. *We've lost the oars, so we can't paddle. Mama and Papa have no idea where we are.* Samantha shivered as tears crept into her eyes. *If only I had not wanted to see Wormley get tarred and feathered*, she thought, *we would not be in this mess.*

She had never felt so sorry for herself as she did at that moment. The storm and the long night without much sleep defeated her efforts to remain awake. Even with the storm roaring, she fell into a fitful sleep. Matthew and James slept too.

When Samantha awoke, the wind had died. The sheets of rain were now only a mist. Samantha crawled out from under the tree trunk and looked around. Waves ran up the shore, but none reached the *Fish Hawk*. Tattered clouds raced across the sky. She woke Matthew and James.

Despite their desperate situation, Samantha smiled at them. "You look like Robinson Crusoe," she laughed.

Matthew replied, "You are certainly not the height of London fashion yourself, Miss Samantha Byrd."

She looked at her soaked clothes. Mud and sand covered her shirt and breeches. "Now that the storm has passed, I'll dry out," she said.

James stared silently at the sky. "The storm is not over," he told them.

"Not over!" Samantha cried. "Look at the sky. Blue is breaking through. The wind has dropped."

James looked at his sister. "Sam," he explained patiently. "This is a hurricane. We are in the eye right now. The center of the storm is always calm. I read that in the almanac."

"What are you talking about?" she grumbled, trying to make sense of what he was saying.

James picked up a stick. He drew a circle in the sand. He made an X.

"This is us," he said pointing to the X. "A hurricane spins around and around, but in the very center it is calm. The front of the storm hit us. It won't be long before the back hits us too."

Samantha didn't want to believe him. Then she remembered the tales that Papa had told of hurricanes striking Virginia: "A hurricane is like a fighter who hits first with one fist and then with the other, while his opponent is still recovering from the first blow."

Samantha took command. "We must get the *Fish Hawk* higher up the beach," she said. "You two push and I'll pull."

The sand held the skiff tightly in its grip. The stranded boat wouldn't budge. Samantha sat down on the bow. She hit her hand against the boat. "Now what?" she asked.

James walked away and came back with a long broken branch.

"This is no time to play," Samantha snarled at him, her patience as exhausted as her muscles.

He ignored her and laid the branch at her feet. He fetched another branch. He set this one three feet ahead of the first. Then he got another and another. By the time he had the fifth branch in place, Samantha realized that he was making rollers.

Together they lifted the bow of the *Fish Hawk* onto the first roller. The sand held the boat tightly, but finally they broke its gritty grip. With a sucking sound the skiff came loose. They slid her along from branch to branch, out of the reach of even the highest wave.

Samantha was curious to see what had been saved inside her boat. But the *Fish Hawk* was too heavy to lift up and flip over.

"James, fetch one more stick, this time a long stout one. Matthew bring a big rock over here." She found two logs of driftwood and rolled them to the side of the boat. With the stick and rock, the boys levered up the skiff. Samantha rolled the logs under the edge. The boys lowered the *Fish Hawk* onto the logs.

Samantha crawled beneath her boat. In the gloom, she saw many things dangling: her water flask, a crab pot, her oyster tongs.

"At least we have shelter for the rest of the storm," she said. "If nothing else, we can catch crabs for food until we're rescued."

"Rescued?" whined James. "Nobody knows where we are, Sam."

"They will come looking for us," she tried to comfort her brother. "Papa and Henry will look for us."

But when? she wondered, as distant thunder cracked to the west.

They huddled under the *Fish Hawk* while the hurricane crashed around them. The pelting of the rain on the boat's bottom was louder than all the militia firing at once. The wind plucked at the boat, trying to flip it over again. It failed. Brief flashes of lightning lit their cave-like world beneath the boat.

Finally, as if defeated in its efforts, the great storm passed. The setting sun broke through the last clouds, its orange glow giving little warmth.

Samantha shook her flask. She shared the water, warning the boys to go sparingly. It was all they had until they could find fresh water somewhere. *But where?* she wondered as she settled down to sleep, her stomach growling. *If only I had stored a round of cheese in the boat. If only . . .*

An osprey's high cry woke Samantha in the morning. She crawled out from beneath the boat. The sun brightened the forest behind them. The James River was almost calm, a slight breeze danced across its surface. *It's just the right breeze to carry us home*, Samantha thought. *If only we had a mast. If only we had a sail.*

Samantha walked to the water's edge. Storm-tossed branches lay in the shallows. Dead crabs and fish lay stranded. She noticed the tide was coming in. She dipped a finger into the water and gave it a taste. Too salty to drink. She licked her lips and kept walking.

The osprey shrieked again and dove into the water. It snatched a fish in its talons and soared back into the sky. *If only we could fish like the osprey,* Samantha thought.

"We can fish!" she said aloud. If her hooks and lines were still in the boat. She turned and ran back to wake James and Matthew. They would go fishing and catch breakfast. After that, she would worry about what to do next.

"Pull, you good for nothing, lazy landlubbers!" ordered a strange voice.

Samantha froze.

Chapter 14

The voice came from beyond a curve in the beach. Samantha dashed to the forest's edge. Stealthily, as if she were stalking a turkey, she slipped along until she could see who had shouted.

Fifty yards offshore was a boat, its bow wedged in the sand.

"Pull!" ordered a tall man standing in the boat. Ten sailors stood in the shallow water, pulling a rope tied in the boat's stern. Samantha was ready to run out when she realized that the man in the boat was British.

Of all the bad luck.

As quietly as she had approached, she retreated. Matthew and James were awake when she returned.

"We're saved," she announced.

The boys look at her as if she'd lost her wits. "Saved?" Matthew asked.

"Sam, who could save us out here?" James said.

"There is another boat just around the point," Samantha explained. "They are stranded in the shallows but soon will have their boat afloat. I'm sure we can ask for their help."

Eagerly, Matthew and James followed Samantha. Hidden in the branches, they watched as the sailors struggled to free their boat.

"They're British boiled crabs!" Matthew exclaimed.

"So," said Samantha. "They might have an extra spar that we can use for a mast. If nothing else, they can give us an ax so we can make a mast."

Matthew stared at his cousin. "Sam," he said. "They are enemy. We are at war with them."

"Matthew, there is no war. Just a bunch of Virginians and Englishmen posturing like fighting roosters. A lot of bluster, but no blood."

"Sam, I'm in the militia. Remember Dunmore's proclamation: All militia are enemies of the King. I could be hanged."

Samantha looked at Matthew. "How will they know you are in the militia if you don't tell them?"

"But, Sam," he protested.

Samantha stomped out of the protection of the forest and onto the beach. "Hullo there, "she yelled.

"Keep pulling, you lily-livered sons of donkeys," yelled the man in the uniform. He stood in the stern urging his men on.

"Hullo there!" Samantha shouted again.

Just then, the sailors pulled especially hard. The boat broke free. Half of the sailors fell backwards into the water. The British officer tumbled tail over teakettle into the boat's bottom. He scrambled to his feet, swearing at his men.

Samantha couldn't help laughing. Seeing the officer fall, on top of all that had happened to her the last few days, released her tension.

The officer scowled at her. He didn't know whether to continue berating his men or to chastise her.

Samantha called, "The storm stranded us. Can you help us?"

"Can't you see I need help myself?" he bellowed at her.

Samantha's temper rose. "Losing your balance is no reason to be rude," she yelled.

The officer brushed himself off. He glared at his men, who quickly wiped the smirks off their faces.

"Watson," he called to one man. "Go find out what she wants." The oldest sailor splashed to shore.

James joined Samantha on the beach.

"Look what the storm's washed up," Watson said. "You are fine, I assume," he said politely, making up for his commanding officer's rudeness.

"Yes," Samantha replied. "But our skiff's mast broke. We saved the sail. Do you have a spar to spare so we could rig a new mast?"

"And some food and water?" begged James.

Watson looked at the bedraggled youngsters. "Storm caught you, eh?"

"Yes," Samantha replied. "Please hurry. Our folks do not know where we are."

"Well, if it was up to me, I'd give you whole blasted tender," Watson told them. "But Lieutenant Jones would most likely object."

He paused before adding, "I'll see what I can do. Whereabouts is your boat?"

"Around that point," Samantha said.

"Wait here," Watson told them, and he dashed back into the water.

"Where's Matthew?" Samantha asked James when Mr. Watson was out of earshot.

"He went back to the *Fish Hawk*. Says he won't have anything to do with the British."

"He is a bigger fool than I thought," Samantha said. "They'll help, enemies or not."

Samantha still couldn't believe that the British were really their enemies. *We are all English, aren't we?* she thought.

Watson returned with water, bread, a round of cheese, and an ax. Samantha took the ax. James grabbed the water, bread, and cheese.

"Lieutenant Jones says you are welcome to the cheese, water, and bread. But he's loaning you the ax," Watson said.

"How will we return it?" Samantha asked.

"Bring it to Norfolk. Ask for Lieutenant Jones of the *Otter*."

"That's one of Dunmore's ships," James blurted out.

Watson eyed him. "That's *Lord* Dunmore to you, son. You wouldn't be rebels, would you? Spying on us?"

"No," Samantha said quickly, pushing James behind her. "We live way up the James on Queen's Creek," she said. "Friends of Thomas Wormley. Maybe you've heard what a good Tory he is." The lie tasted bitter. "We were fishing off Burleigh's Landing. The storm caught us and swept us along."

"We don't live—"James began to say.

Samantha kicked him.

Watson scratched his head. "Makes no never mind to me," he said. "Just return the ax, or he'll take it out of my pay."

"Watson! Conclude your business," Lieutenant Jones shouted. "We must get under way."

"Thank you very much," Samantha said sincerely.

"Thank you," James echoed.

Without another word, Watson returned to his boat. As it pulled away, Samantha read the name *Eagle* on its stern.

"Nice craft, that," she said admiringly as the *Eagle*'s sail filled. "Come on," she said to James. "We have work to do."

"But Sam," James said, "why did you tell him we were from Queen's Creek? We live on College Creek."

"So he can look there for his ax," she explained. She hefted the sharp blade.

Matthew was leaning against the *Fish Hawk*.

"Let's eat before we look for a new mast," Samantha suggested.

Matthew snatched the cheese from James's hand. He looked it over. "This cheese came from Papa's store," he exclaimed. "I can tell by the seal. They must have stolen it off an American boat. Papa would never sell cheese to the boiled crabs."

"Who cares?" Samantha said. "It's cheese. And we're hungry."

"I care," Matthew stormed. "I won't have anything to do with pirated food."

Samantha was tired. She didn't have the energy to battle Matthew over the cheese. She didn't care if it had fallen off the moon, she was going to enjoy it. "Suit yourself," she said. She took her knife and sliced off two big chunks. One, she handed to James. The other, she ate with a piece of soggy bread. She drank her fill of water too.

Then, taking the ax, she walked down the shore. Finding the right tree for the mast was not difficult. The storm had uprooted and toppled so many trees that she had her pick of the best. Choosing a young oak sapling, she trimmed off the branches and dragged it back to the *Fish Hawk*.

While she worked on the mast, Matthew and James spread the two parts of the sail out to dry. Samantha looked them over. She picked the biggest half to use. This she attached to the new mast with its old fittings.

Using the lever and rock, they turned the *Fish Hawk* over so she rested on her bottom. The stump of the mast was still firmly in place. Using all of the rope she could spare, Samantha lashed the new mast to what was left of the old. "Let's get her down to the water," she ordered. Using James's roller logs, they pushed and pulled the *Fish Hawk* to the water's edge.

The tide was high. Soon the *Fish Hawk* was afloat. They climbed aboard. Samantha raised the makeshift sail.

"It's not pretty," she said as the wind filled the sail. "But it will get us home."

The *Fish Hawk* limped up College Creek just as the moon rose.

Mama stood alone on the wharf. "Thank God you are safe," she said, her soft words carrying across the water.

Chapter 15

"Mama, you should have heard the thunder and seen the lightning," James chattered before they touched shore. "We turned over and our mast broke and—"

"Whoa, James," Mama said. "You can tell me when we are inside."

Samantha eased the *Fish Hawk* into the wharf. She looked for Papa amid the broken branches that littered the farmyard. She didn't know what kind of greeting to expect from him

Mama said, "Boys, change into dry clothes while I get supper. It's a fine stew that's been cooking—for two days." Mama looked sternly at Samantha. "Wait here, young lady," she said. She stirred the big kettle on the fire. The smell of steaming stew made Samantha's mouth water. She licked her lips in anticipation.

"I have one question. I want the answer before Papa returns," Mama told her. "Was it your idea to take off in the *Fish Hawk* into the James River?"

"Yes, Mama," Samantha answered in her meekest voice.

"As I thought," Mama said, setting three wooden bowls on the table. She rattled three spoons as she laid them down. "Child, when will you ever use that common sense I know you were born with?" Mama asked.

She did not expect an answer. But Samantha had one ready. "Mama, we were only going to see the tar and feathering. But Papa beat us home, and we were going to act as if we had gotten up early to go fishing." Samantha's meekness melted. "I didn't expect a hurricane, Mama!"

Mama came to Samantha and put her arms around her. Samantha snuggled against her warmth. "I know, Samantha," Mama soothed. "I know. But how is it that you get yourself into so much trouble without even trying?"

"Trouble just has a way of finding me, I guess."

Mama released her and gave her a love pat. "Get out of those clothes. Tomorrow will be a big washing day," she sighed.

Nobody was more surprised than Mama when Samantha came out of her room dressed in her dress. Mama burst out laughing, "Samantha Byrd, if you don't take all!"

James hardly paused to swallow as he told Mama about their adventure. Mama nodded her head and refilled the bowls as they were rapidly emptied.

Samantha was anxious to find out where Papa and Henry were. But the chance didn't come until James had laid his head down on the table and fallen asleep.

"Leave him be," Mama said. "He'll wake soon enough when Papa returns."

"When might that be?" Samantha asked eagerly.

"I've been expecting him all along," Mama said. "He took old Jasper and went looking for you three on land. Henry borrowed a boat and went searching on the James."

"We didn't see him," Matthew said.

"I guessed that," Mama replied. "Said he would look east along the peninsula and come back west up the Norfolk shore. He figured you would run to safety and wait out the storm."

"Samantha did try, Aunt Maggie," Matthew said. "She really did. But the waves were monstrously big."

"What I don't understand is why the British sailors helped you." Mama said.

Samantha had been chewing on that same thought herself.

"Mama, I think that when there's a big danger, all the little dangers don't add up to anything much. Folks just help one another no matter their differences."

Mama looked at Samantha as if she just announced she was going to wear a dress every day for the rest of her life.

"Maybe something good has come out of your traipsing around," Mama said. "You are growing up."

They had been so intent on their talk that they did not hear Jasper's hoofbeats. Papa burst into the room like a gust of hurricane wind. "They have Henry!" he exclaimed, standing in the doorway.

"Who has Henry?" Mama cried.

"A blasted bunch of British!" Papa shouted. He glared at Samantha. "He was out looking for you and got himself captured."

Samantha broke down. It had all been too much: the storm, the shipwreck, the sail home. Now Henry captured because of her. Tears erupted and flowed down her cheeks. She didn't even try to stop them. This was all her fault!

If only she was dead none of this would have happened.

If only.

Chapter 16

Samantha slept fitfully. As tired as she was, knowing that Henry had been captured because of her made her toss and turn all night. Martha gave up trying to sleep beside her and slept in the chair by the fireplace.

In the morning, Samantha would not look anyone in the eyes. Breakfast was solemn: Each person was wrapped up in his or her thoughts.

After breakfast Samantha and Matthew went down to the dock. The sight of the *Fish Hawk* made Samantha want to start crying all over again. It looked like the wreck it was—the broken mast, the mud and sand sticking to the gunwales, the tangle of fishing gear.

"I'll help you," Matthew said and went to work emptying the boat. Without a word, Samantha joined him. First she cut loose the oak branch that she had used for a mast. After taking off the sail and the pulley for raising it, she tossed the branch into the creek. It drifted slowly downstream. She got a bucket and washed the gunwales.

Matthew spread her things out to dry. He untangled her fishing line and recoiled it in its wooden tub. Using twine, he mended a cracked lathe of her crab pot.

The air was still. Samantha's heron friend called, "Kraannkk," as it flew in search of a better feeding ground. Butterflies flitted from flower to flower. A fish jumped for a bug and landed with a soft splash. Behind the barn, Papa chopped wood.

Samantha looked around the farm. She was embarrassed that she hadn't even asked how they weathered the storm. Shingles had blown off of Mama's henhouse. The barn door hung askew. Otherwise, the buildings looked normal. Except for the blackened pile of the tobacco shed.

Her thoughts drifted to Henry. All morning she hadn't been able to face thinking of him. *Where was he? How was he being treated? Would they hang him for being a rebel?* He was wearing his hunting shirt, a sure symbol of his allegiance to Virginia, not the King. *What is Papa going to do?*

As if he heard her thoughts, Papa came from behind the barn. He was carrying a new mast! "Samantha," he said, "fetch an ax. We'll need to get rid of this stump before we can set the new mast."

She handed him the ax she had borrowed from the British. Papa chopped out the old mast stump. Samantha ran her fingers down the long, smooth new mast. She fastened the pulley close to the top. She was almost happy. Then she remembered Henry.

"Matthew. Run tell Aunt Maggie we're ready," said Papa. Matthew dashed to the house.

What does Mama have to do with my boat? Samantha wondered.

Papa put his hands on Samantha's shoulders. She looked at the ground. He raised her chin so she had to look him in the eyes. "Sam, I am sorry for what I said last night. I was angry. I still am. But I am angry that my actions placed the three of you in danger."

But, Papa—" she interrupted.

"Hush, Sam. Don't argue with me." He stroked her hair. "In my anger at Thomas Wormley, I meant to harm him. If I hadn't been such a hothead and gone to tar and feather him, you three would never have stolen out. The rest wouldn't have happened either. But now you're safe. We just need to find Henry."

Samantha opened her mouth to speak. Papa placed a finger over it.

"Your mother and I talked about this long into the night. Mama and I have decided to help you repair the *Fish Hawk*. Then we will sail to Williamsburg to learn what we can about Henry."

Papa looked past Samantha. Mama was carrying the *Fish Hawk*'s old sails, newly stitched.

"Even as much as Mama is opposed to your traipsing around like a boy, she knows how much this boat means to you. And Sam, she really appreciates all the hard work you do."

Tears welled up. Samantha wiped her eyes.

Matthew trailed Mama, carrying Samantha's musket and his.

Samantha hugged Papa and Mama.

"Now, child," Mama said, "no sense in making such a fuss. We have work to do."

In an hour, the repaired sail was rigged on the new mast. Samantha's gear was stowed. She placed the British ax with her other gear. The *Fish Hawk* was shipshape once again.

Samantha admired her boat. She laughed when she saw Mama coming to the dock, a basket under her arm. Martha and James followed.

"We're ready," Mama said.

Samantha could not believe it. Mama was going to sail in her boat. She had never set foot in the *Fish Hawk* before. Neither had Martha. For the longest time nothing ever happened to me, Samantha thought, and now my whole world is upside down. Things would be perfect if only Henry were here. Then she remembered her brother's predicament. Her thoughts turned to getting them to Williamsburg as quickly as possible.

The *Fish Hawk* was crowded. Mama and Martha sat in the bow. James, Matthew, and Papa sat along the sides. Samantha sat in the stern, guiding her boat with the tiller. The morning breeze moved up College Creek. With the wind at her back, the *Fish Hawk* moved confidently.

Samantha pointed out her favorite places to Mama,

who showed a genuine interest. The sail would have been most pleasant if her thoughts hadn't kept flickering to Henry. What could she do to help him?

Nothing, if Lord Dunmore had impressed him into service on one of his ships. Samantha knew from listening to the adults talk that all impressed Americans were watched like criminals to make sure they did not escape. *Why can't the darn British use their own sailors? Why can't they leave the Virginians and other colonists alone? It isn't fair*, she thought.

They tied up at Uncle John's wharf.

"I'll take Samantha and James to Sarah's house," Mama announced. "I know you have business to discuss with John." She paused. "Bring any word about Henry to us immediately."

Samantha was about to protest and say that she wanted to be with Papa. However, she was determined to be on her best behavior. She even thought about wearing her dress—if Mama hadn't left it at home. Samantha secretly hoped she had.

Samantha pulled Matthew aside and whispered, "You listen to every word they say. I want to know what's happening."

Matthew agreed and said his goodbyes. He ran home to let his family know that Papa was coming.

Mama had not forgotten the dress, but she didn't press Samantha to wear it. After greetings were made and the news of Henry's capture was shared, Mama placed the dress in the wardrobe, where it stayed between visits to town.

Martha, Mama, and Sarah chatted while preparing dinner. Samantha played with her little cousins, helping with dinner when she was asked to. Sarah appreciated the break from her brood.

Papa returned with Uncle John as the clock chimed one. Everyone waited anxiously for Papa to speak. "Henry was captured by a tender from the *Otter*," he said.

"We know that ship," Samantha blurted out.

Papa's look silenced her.

"Henry and four other men were taken aboard yesterday morning. A militiaman who was almost captured himself saw them. He traveled through the night to bring word to Williamsburg." Papa stopped and looked directly at Mama. "All we can do is pray he will not be harmed for being a rebel. And that he can escape."

Silence fell on the room. Uncle John finally broke it. "However," he said. "I have a plan to rescue Henry."

All eyes turned toward him. Samantha's gaze was as intense as if she were sighting a shot at a deer.

"Today is the sixth of September. The last day I can ship tobacco to England is the tenth. I refuse to have anything to do with the English, deadline or not. I am taking my ship to Saint Eustatius. There I'll sell my tobacco and other products to the Dutch. I'll fill the *Cardinal*'s hold with gunpowder and bring her back in six weeks."

Papa cleared his throat and looked straight at Mama again. "John has offered to take James on his ship as cabin boy."

Chapter 17

Samantha leaped to her feet.

"James!" she cried. "Why he doesn't know the bow of a boat from the stern!"

Everyone looked at her as if she had exploded a squib on the table.

"Sit down, young lady," Papa commanded. Whenever Papa called her young lady, she knew he would brook no argument. She sat down.

Mama spoke up. "Why on earth should he sail as a cabin boy?" she asked. "It's far too risky."

Uncle John said, "Maggie, the *Cardinal* is as safe as Samantha's *Fish Hawk*."

Samantha flinched when he said that. He must not yet know of their mishaps on the *Fish Hawk*.

"It will be good for the boy," Papa said. "He is always

so eager to learn. Let him learn at sea. It will make a man of him. Look how Matthew changed after he sailed on the *Cardinal*."

Samantha thought that Matthew was always the same. Had she missed something?

James sat silently through this discussion. Samantha looked at him. *Where's your backbone?* she wondered. *Speak for yourself. Tell them no.*

"I'll go," James said. "It will be . . . an adventure!"

Samantha wanted to punch him. Her luck was going from bad to worse. She, the sailor in the family, should be sailing with Uncle John.

Her next thought struck like a hammer. She couldn't sail with Uncle John anyway. She was a girl. *If only I were a boy*, she thought. *If only.*

Mama was arguing with Papa and Uncle John, but she was losing. Even as strong-minded as Mama was, Papa usually got his way in the end.

"Maggie, it is settled. James sails on the tenth of September with John." Papa crossed his arms. The decision was final.

Samantha piped up. "Uncle John, you said you had a plan to rescue Henry."

Uncle John looked at Papa. Papa shook his head. "Mama and I will discuss his plan later. Alone." He looked directly at Samantha.

After dinner the talk turned to the fighting between the Americans and the British. Samantha excused herself and went outside. She wandered aimlessly through the streets of Williamsburg. She gazed into the various shops. Her thoughts were not on what she saw but on James's sailing with Uncle John. *If only I weren't a girl, I would get to go too*, she thought, kicking a tree.

Her wanderings took her down Market Street to a long, open park. Looking down the park, she saw the Governor's Palace. *Goodbye to you, Lord Dunmore*, she thought. *And good riddance. You've caused me and my family enough trouble.*

Then she remembered something that Mama had told her: "Never trouble trouble, till trouble troubles you. For if you trouble trouble, trouble is sure to trouble you."

"I would like to trouble your trouble, Lord Dunmore," Samantha said out loud.

"I'm sure he is scared," someone laughed.

Samantha's face flushed as she spun around to see who her tormentor was.

Matthew!

"You scoundrel!" she said. "Listening in on someone's private thoughts."

"If they are so private, you should keep them in your head," he teased. "Anyway, I know a secret."

"I do too," Samantha replied.

"You first," Matthew said.

Samantha looked around. "Let's go by that tree."

When they were seated in the shade Samantha said, "Your father is taking James with him aboard the *Cardinal* when he sails to Saint Eustatius."

Matthew laughed. "That's no secret. Papa told me. And besides, I am going too."

"You're what?" Samantha cried.

"I'm sailing with them too," Matthew bragged.

"But you are in the militia. You can't go." What she really wanted to say was, "If I can't go, you can't go."

"Papa talked with Sergeant Shell. He dismissed me from the militia until I return. After all, I have sailed before."

"But it's not fair," Samantha snapped. "Why can't I go?"

Matthew stared at her. The answer was obvious.

"You males get to do everything. We females just have to stay home and cook, tend the gardens, spin the thread, make the candles, do the wash . . ."

"There's more to it, Sam," he said. "This is the real secret. But you have to promise not to tell anyone."

"Promises are like piecrust," Samantha said. "Easy to make and easy to break."

"Then I won't share this. It is too important."

Samantha turned to her cousin. "I've never broken a promise between us, Matthew. Why should I start now?"

"Because you are so angry, Sam. And this will make you angrier."

Samantha ached to know what the secret was, but she didn't want to give in.

Matthew stood to leave.

"I promise," she whispered.

He sat back down and leaned toward her. "Papa is not really sailing with a load of tobacco and pine planks. He's not taking any trade goods with him."

"Why ever not?" she asked. "What is he going to use to trade to the Dutch for the gunpowder?"

"Sam, he's not even sailing to the Caribbean," Matthew answered. "He's only sailing down into Chesapeake Bay."

"Whatever for?" she asked.

"To capture British ships!" Matthew said. "Papa has a letter of marque."

"Whatever is a letter of marque?" Samantha asked.

"It is a special letter saying that Papa can legally capture British ships."

"Why does he need a letter? Why can't he just capture them?"

"We're not really at war yet, Sam. Without the letter of marque, Papa would be a pirate like Blackbeard. With it, he has permission to attack British ships. The *Cardinal* is going to be a privateer."

Samantha sat silently, digesting Matthew's words. "You and James are going to be pirates?"

"Not pirates. Privateers. And we get a share of all the ships we capture."

"A share?"

"When the ship is sold, all of the pirates—I mean privateers—split the prize money. James and I will be rich. And your father too.`

"Papa? Why?"

"He's given my father all his money to buy a share of my father's ship. That way, he gets a share of the prize money too."

Suddenly Samantha understood Uncle John's and Papa's plans. Uncle John would try to capture the ship that Henry was on so he could rescue Henry. Then he would sell the ship. Papa would get enough money to buy the land and send James to William and Mary.

Samantha wanted to scream at the top of her lungs, "And I'll be at home!"

She tugged her hat down over her unruly hair and tucked the loose strands under to keep them out of her face. She was so frustrated that she felt like cutting off her hair.

Like a bolt of lightning, an idea struck her: I will cut off my hair. And I'll sail in James's place aboard the *Cardinal!*

Chapter 18

Samantha debated whether to include Matthew in her plans. She looked at her cousin as he watched two dogs fight across the green. He could be trusted not to tell Mama and Papa. But what if he thought it was a bad idea and would not help her?

She would do it on her own.

She walked back to Sarah's house. She listened for the sound of Matthew's feet behind her. She willed herself not to turn around to see if was following her.

He wasn't, and she walked alone to Sarah's.

Her family was saying their goodbyes. Samantha forced a smile onto her face. Outside, she looked as if nothing was wrong. Inside, she boiled like a steaming kettle of crabs.

"We will join you in three days at Burleigh's Landing,"

Papa told Uncle John.

"Be prompt. I'll sail on the tide's turning on the tenth."

"I will be there, Uncle John," James piped up. "Rain or shine."

Samantha wanted to kick him for his cheerfulness. Who did he think he was, sailing on the *Cardinal* without her? Didn't anyone know how unfair this whole idea was? She should be aboard the *Cardinal* when it sailed, not lily-livered James.

On the sail home, James chattered about the great things he would do aboard the *Cardinal*. He would learn to sail a great ship, not a little skiff. He would learn the names of every fish and bird he saw. He would . . .

Samantha finally managed to block out his words.

Mama, looking severe, sat in the stern with Samantha. She didn't say a word the entire trip.

Samantha hardly noticed the watery world around them. A blue heron winged its way overhead. She paid no attention. Fish splashed. She ignored them. A muskrat family failed to divert her. A flock of geese, looking for a winter refuge, honked overhead. She barely heard them. Normally, she would have watched where they landed, figuring she and Henry would hunt them.

Samantha mulled a plan in her head. She would disguise herself as James. She glanced at her twin brother. Every day of her life she had seen him. Now she looked at him with different eyes. She noticed how he held his hand to his eyes to shield them from the sun. She watched his expressions as he talked about being a cabin boy. She saw how he straightened his queue.

She'd have to cut off about half of her hair and tie it in a queue. That would be easy. Imitating James would be easy too. She'd only have to pretend until they were well out in the bay, too far to bother to return her to shore. She'd let Mama and Papa know what she planned to do so they wouldn't worry about her. She would leave them a note, so they would not worry too much.

But how in the world will I stop James from going aboard the Cardinal? she wondered. *How will I take his place?*

Samantha was so deep in thought that she almost sailed past their landing. A nudge from Mama's elbow brought her back to the here and now.

"Child, put your mind on what's at hand," Mama said.

Samantha tacked and turned her boat so it slid up to the wharf. She handed things to Papa while Mama and Martha went into the house to begin making supper. Cheerily, James watered Jasper. Samantha heard him chattering as she straightened ropes, stowed her fishing gear back aboard, and rolled up her sail.

All the while, she struggled with the problem of keeping James back while she sailed on the *Cardinal.* She could tie him to a tree. But he would holler for help. She could gag him and tie him to a tree. But who would know where to find him and untie him? She could take him fishing and leave him stranded on an island. But who would rescue him? She could pray he got sick and could not go . . . What was she going to do? She *had* to sail with

Uncle John and rescue Henry.

Supper was quiet after Mama barked at James to leave off with his chatter. Mama's looks at Papa were as cold as icicles. Martha ate and excused herself. Samantha felt like a volcano ready to explode, but she forced herself to keep the lid on. Any outbursts would doom her plans.

Samantha watched the way James held his knife as he ate with it. She noticed how he held his cup as he drank. She watched as he broke his bread and ate it, carefully catching any crumbs on his plate. She had seen him do these things many times before, but it was if she were watching them for the first time.

Samantha glanced at Mama. She wasn't glaring at Papa, but she had an eye on Samantha. *I can't let on about what I am thinking*, Samantha told herself.

Even as she lay in bed that night, Samantha struggled with how to take James's place. *If only Henry were here*, she thought, *he would know what to do.*

Her thoughts focused on Henry. At least they knew where he was. She felt relieved that Thomas Wormley had not taken action against him. From the stories she had heard, Henry's life would be unpleasant: cramped space, wormy food, and the awful smell of bilge water. But what Henry probably missed most was his freedom.

"Hold on, Henry," Samantha whispered. "I am coming." *But how?* she worried as she fell asleep.

An owl hooted, "Whoooo—oo."

Its mate answered, "Whooo-oo-oo."

Chapter 18

At the sound of the owls, Samantha sat bolt upright.
While she had slept, her brain had solved her puzzle.
She knew how to get aboard Uncle John's privateer.

Chapter 19

She would need James to help. If he went along with her plan, both could sail on the *Cardinal!*

Samantha wanted to rush up the ladder to the loft and shake him awake. She knew she couldn't do that without rousing the whole household, though. She tossed and turned so much that Martha woke up and bid her to be still.

Samantha rolled over and pulled the cloth plug from the hole in the wall. Peeking out, she tracked the moon as it set. She lay as still as a log until the night faded and dawn came.

She woke James and whispered for him to follow her. Rubbing the sleep from his eyes, he trailed behind Samantha to the wharf. No one could overhear them there.

"I am going on the *Cardinal*," she announced.

"What? Sam, you can't go. I'm going."

"Hush and listen. We are both going."

James stared at his sister in astonishment. Her hands were on her hips. He knew that when she stood like that her mind was made up and nothing would change it. She was just like Mama and Papa.

"How?" he asked, now curious.

Samantha grabbed his arm, and he fell silent.

"I'm going to cut my hair to look like yours. We're going to dress the same. You will go onto the ship as planned. I am going to sneak aboard."

"But the captain will know."

"No, he won't. We are twins, aren't we? When we dress alike, no one will be able to tell us apart, especially if I act like you."

Samantha leaped off the wharf and picked a flower. She twisted it one way and then the other as she studied it. "This is a pickerelweed," she said in perfect imitation of James.

Her brother smiled, then laughed. "Is that really what I look like?"

It was Samantha's turn to laugh. "Yes."

"We can trade being cabin boy," James said, getting into the act now. "I can hide while you are cabin boy and you can do the same." A worried look crossed his face. "But what if we get caught?"

"We only have to get so far out into the bay that the captain will not want to bother to sail back and put me ashore. After that it won't matter."

"What about Mama and Papa?"

"Papa will be taking you to the landing. I will leave Mama a note explaining what we are doing and how we are going to help rescue Henry. By the time she reads it, we will both be gone."

"How will you get to the landing?"

"In the *Fish Hawk*."

"I don't know, Sam," James said, beginning to waver.

"Well, if you don't help me, I swear I'll tie you to a tree and leave you until Papa finds you. By then the *Cardinal* will have sailed."

James knew by the intensity in her voice that Samantha meant what she said.

"What clothes will you wear?" James asked.

Samantha thought for a moment. "Our breeches are nearly the same, so that won't make much difference. You'll have to smuggle out a shirt for me. We both have hats." She took hers off and ran her hand over her long red hair.

"I'll wait until the last minute to cut my hair. I'll tie it in a queue like yours. With my hat on, no one will be able to tell us apart."

She tried to sound more sure of herself than she was. Her plan was a desperate one. But she was desperate. Wasn't it her fault that Henry had been captured? Then it was her responsibility to rescue him. This was her only chance.

"Let's do our chores as we always do," she said. "James,

remember, not a word to anyone. Act naturally. If you spoil this, I'll tie you up anyway!"

"Sam, don't worry," he assured her. "We can do this."

James fed Jasper while Samantha gathered eggs. She slopped her pig with scraps from the table. She milked Molly, their cow. While her hands squeezed Molly's teats and warm milk squirted into the bucket, Samantha's brain turned her plan over and over, trying to find a flaw.

"As long as James doesn't give us away," she told Molly, "I'll rescue Henry."

When James and Samantha entered the house after their chores, Mama said, "I wondered when you two would be finished."

Papa said, "Son, you'll have to be faster when the ship's captain gives an order. You can't lollygag around and daydream."

"Yes, Papa," James said. "I have a lot to learn."

Samantha said nothing as she ate.

Mama eyed her suspiciously. "Cat got your tongue?" she asked.

"No, I was thinking," Samantha answered.

"About what?" Papa asked.

"About where the best fishing might be this morning."

"May I go with you?" James asked.

Samantha usually refused his requests to come along when she fished. James was so clumsy in a boat. But if he were with her, he couldn't accidentally blurt out her plans.

"Yes, come with me," Samantha said. "You can practice being my cabin boy." She said it harshly, as she did when she teased him, to keep Mama from suspecting that she was up to something.

The days passed quickly. James slipped out a shirt. Samantha hid it in a canvas bag along with other things she had collected. She watched as Mama, now resigned to letting James go, helped him fill his bag. In it she placed a needle and thread, a spare pair of stockings, an extra shirt, and a second blue neckerchief.

Secretly, Samantha took the same things and placed them in her bag. She hoped that the captain would not be very observant of a lowly cabin boy. She frequently ran her fingers through her hair, knowing it soon would be gone.

On the morning of James's departure, Samantha packed the *Fish Hawk*. As soon as Papa and James were off to the landing, she'd sail.

After breakfast Mama hugged James. Tears slipped from the corners of her eyes. She wiped them away. Martha hugged James too.

"Come home safely," Mama said before turning back to the house.

Samantha watched her go. Mama's shoulders sagged, as if she were carrying a great weight. Henry was gone, and now James. Samantha hated to add to her mother's burden, but she had no choice. She had to rescue Henry.

Samantha hugged James too. She whispered, "Don't act surprised when you see me. I'll get aboard somehow."

Out loud she said, "And don't fall overboard."

James grinned. "I won't. The *Cardinal* is ever so much bigger than your *Fish Hawk*."

James climbed up behind Papa, and they set off for the

10-mile ride to Burleigh's Landing.

Samantha followed Martha and Mama into the house. She pretended to busy herself mending a rip in one of Papa's shirts. She slipped the scissors into her pocket.

"I think I'll set my crab pots now," she said.

Mama held out her hand. "You won't need my scissors crabbing," she said.

Chapter 20

Samantha handed Mama the scissors. "I don't know what I was thinking," she said innocently.

Mama looked at her peculiarly.

Samantha went to the door. "I am going downstream to set my traps. I'll be home for dinner." *I hate to do this to you, Mama*, Samantha said in her head, *but I have to.*

Last night, while everyone was helping James prepare, Samantha slipped to her room and wrote a note to Mama and Papa. She had it tucked inside her shirt. It read:

Mama and Papa,

Please don't be too angry with me. I sailed with the *Cardinal* to find Henry. It is my fault he was captured. I must try to rescue him. I will be home safely at the end of the voyage. I promise.

Your loving daughter, Samantha.

Samantha hurried to the barn. She placed the note in Jasper's water bucket, where Papa would find it.

As she cast off the *Fish Hawk*, Samantha glanced toward her house. Mama stood in the doorway, holding Samantha's musket. Why did Mama have to find her gun? Now Mama might suspect she was up to something.

"I'm just going crabbing," she shouted. "I don't need it."

"Samantha, where are you going?" Mama called.

Samantha ignored her mother's cry and raised the sails. The *Fish Hawk* glided into the creek.

"Samantha Byrd!" Mama yelled.

Samantha tightened the sheet until the sail was as taut as she felt inside. Then she and the *Fish Hawk* disappeared around a bend.

At a secluded place further along, Samantha pulled to shore. She took almost everything out of the *Fish Hawk*: her crab pots, coils of fishing line, oyster tongs, ax. The sight of the ax made her hesitate. Could she cut her hair with it? She licked her thumb and ran her finger along the blade. It was sharp enough.

Throwing her hat on the ground, she reached behind and bunched her long hair together. Holding the ax in one hand and her hair in the other, she rubbed her hair against the blade. At first only a few strands were cut. She tightened her grip on her hair and bore down on the blade. She cut until her hand swung free, a foot of red tresses dangling from it.

Samantha went to the *Fish Hawk* and pulled out an

old piece of sailcloth. She gently wrapped her hair in it and hid the bundle with her other belongings. Then she twisted her remaining hair into a rat's tail and tied it with twine. Now she had a queue like James's. She put on her hat, climbed into her boat, and set sail for Burleigh's Landing.

Samantha's thoughts were jumbled. She didn't want to hurt Mama. But she had to help Henry. What if she got caught like Henry? What if James got caught too? Maybe she shouldn't go through with her idea. "I must find Henry," she repeated over and over.

Samantha saw Burleigh's Landing. The *Cardinal*, tied to the wharf, was immense compared to the *Fish Hawk*. The *Cardinal*'s single mast towered above its deck. The bowsprit lunged forward like the spear of a swordfish. Samantha counted two cannons, one in the bow and the other in the stern. With only two cannons, she thought, how will the *Cardinal* ever fight the British?

For the first time, Samantha realized that she had chosen sides. She was going to sail against the British. Maybe even fight. No matter what, I will not fire upon them, she promised herself.

A sudden gust of wind made the *Fish Hawk* heel and brought Samantha's attention back to her boat. She couldn't just sail up to the wharf, hop out, and climb aboard the *Cardinal*. She had to create a plan quickly. She had been worrying so much about Mama and Henry that she had not planned what she would do when she reached Burleigh's Landing.

She came about and sailed back the way she had come. Once out of sight, she looked for a place to land. She thought about hiding the *Fish Hawk* up a small creek and going overland but dismissed that idea almost as soon as it had taken shape. Trudging through the swamps and marshes would be impossible. What if she missed the *Cardinal's* sailing?

She looked at the sun. It had swung past noon. Papa and James should be arriving soon. What if she waited until nearly sunset? That would give James and Matthew time to settle aboard, and by then their fathers would be on their separate ways home. At sunset she would sail past the wharf and up Queen's Creek. She'd land somewhere near the road and reach Burleigh's Landing that way.

The afternoon stretched on and on. The sun beat down on Samantha. She filled her hat with water and dumped it over her head. The cool water brought some relief. It felt odd not having her long hair hanging down her back. She wished she had remembered to bring along food. By suppertime she was starving. But each time she felt sorry for herself, she repeated, "I must help Henry. I must help Henry."

As the huge orange ball of the sun was setting, Samantha turned the *Fish Hawk* toward the landing. The wind pushed her along. She gazed in wonder again at the *Cardinal.* Samantha could hardly believe she was going to sail on her. She waved at some sailors watching her pass. She kept her distance, though, so no one would recognize her boat.

A mile upstream she guided the *Fish Hawk* into the mouth of a small creek. The tide was out, and she ran the bow up on shore. She furled the sails. Then, grabbing her canvas bag in one hand and the painter in the other, she leaped into the black mud. It squished to the tops of her moccasins. Squelching through it, she tied her boat securely to a tree. She struck the road and turned south. The setting sun peeked through the trees as she stopped and stared at the *Cardinal*.

How I am going to get aboard? she wondered.

Chapter 21

Samantha watched three sailors standing in the bow, smoking their pipes. Another sailor stood by the gangway.

She looked at the village of Burleigh's Landing. She could make out a few buildings in the dim light. A door opened, and a shaft of light fell on a swinging sign. Even from a distance, Samantha could tell it was the Boar's Head Tavern. Sounds of laughter and singing drifted on the evening air. The door closed and the sounds died away.

Samantha walked to the tavern. Several wagons were drawn up in front of the tavern. She gasped. One was Papa's wagon. She recognized the eagle branded into its side—the eagle that stood for the Byrd family, and that was stamped on all of Papa's tobacco hogsheads.

Samantha slipped behind the tavern. Papa hadn't gone home. In spite of the heat, she shivered. That meant that

Mama did not know where she was, for Papa wouldn't have seen the note yet. "Please forgive me, Mama," Samantha whispered.

If Papa was staying the night, then where was James? Was he still with Papa, waiting to go aboard the *Cardinal* in the morning? Or was he already on board? There was only way to find out. She would approach the sailor on guard duty. If he stopped her, then he didn't know James. If he let her through, he knew James.

Samantha hitched up her breeches. She brushed her shirt. She reached up to stuff her hair under her hat. When she grabbed the queue she remembered that her long hair was gone. She pulled her hat down tighter on her head. She took a deep breath.

Good luck, she thought, remembering something that Henry had told her long ago: "Luck is a very good word, if you put a p in front of it."

Well, if nothing else, this will take plenty of pluck, she thought.

As she neared the *Cardinal*, Samantha walked straight ahead, as if she had business onboard. A bell chimed the hour. A sailor called out, "Eight bells. Give the glass a turn, Matthew."

"Aye-aye, sir," he called. Samantha felt relieved. Matthew was on the ship. But what about James?

Samantha walked up the gangway. "Halt," the sailor on guard duty said. "Who might you be?" He held up a lantern. The beam fell across her face. "Oh, young James Byrd," he smiled. "I thought you was below."

"I needed to tend to some last minute business for my

114

father before we sailed," Samantha said.

"You'd best hang your hammock now, lad," the sailor said. "We sail on the tide's change at first light."

"Thank you," she said politely as she passed. "I'll do so immediately."

She turned toward the stern.

The sailor laughed. "Master James," he said, "you are not the captain yet. You berth before the mast."

"Oh," Samantha replied, scratching her chin. "I plumb forgot." She wanted to talk with Matthew, who stood near the wheel at the stern. Now she would have to wait.

She changed directions and walked towards the bow. Ahead she saw a hatch with a ladder leading down. Voices rose from the opening. Gingerly, she placed a foot on the first step. Before she could take another, she heard James's voice.

"Give me back my book!" he cried.

"Give me back my book!" an echoing voice mimicked James.

Samantha was about to plunge down the hatch and throttle whoever was tormenting her brother, but that would give her away. Instead, she slid from the opening. Hugging her canvas bag, she ducked behind a gun carriage to plan her next move. James would have to defend himself.

Her attention was drawn to an opening door. Three men stepped out onto the deck.

"See that you keep our sons out of harm's way," one said. Samantha recognized the voice as Uncle John's.

115

"Captain Black, my thanks again for taking James on this voyage," Papa said. "He's a lad with plenty of book learning but not much experience."

Samantha stifled a giggle. With Samantha sharing his duties, James was going to be twice the person anyone expected.

The third voice rumbled like gravel on a creek bed. "As long as they do their duties and follow orders, they'll do fine," said Captain Black.

"Keep a wary eye open for Dunmore's naval ships," Uncle John warned.

"Never you fear, Mr. Byrd. Me lads have been watching them from ship and shore for nigh on a month. There's not much that misses their eyes."

And watch for Henry! Samantha wanted to call out. Papa beat her to it. "We especially want news of the *Otter*."

Captain Black said, "I'll try, but there's no guaranteeing she'll be out of Newport Harbor. I can't sail in under the British guns and waylay her."

"Do your best is all we ask," Papa said.

"Gentlemen, you have my word," said Captain Black. "Dunmore's impressed four of my finest men. Snatched them right off the streets of Newport. I want them back, or I'll get my revenge. And now, good night. Time and tide wait for no man. We sail at dawn."

"May God go with you," Papa said.

"And a fair wind fill your sails," added Uncle John.

The door closed behind Captain Black. Samantha

drew farther back into the shadows as Papa and Uncle John passed her hiding place. They crossed the gangway. Their boots crunched across the oyster shells that paved the road. A shaft of light spilled onto the street as they entered the tavern.

Samantha waited for the *Cardinal*'s crew to settle. Rumbling snores soon came from below. She peered around the gun carriage. The guard had pulled in the gangplank, and he now sat slumped on a barrel. Matthew paced the deck at the stern, pausing every so often to open the shade on his lantern and look at the hourglass.

Samantha waited until Matthew had struck two bells—nine o'clock—before leaving her hiding place. She was glad now that she had paid attention when Uncle John had explained a few things about shipboard life to James.

Sticking to the shadows, she ducked under the long boom. For a joke, she wanted to startle Matthew by suddenly appearing out of the dark. But he might yell out an alarm. This is no time to play, she reminded herself. The *Cardinal* was now a ship of war, and Samantha was sailing aboard her.

"Matthew," she whispered.

He jumped at the sound of her voice. She stepped out of the shadows.

"James," he hissed. "You've frightened me out of a year's growth. Don't ever do that again."

He doesn't recognize me, Samantha thought. She decided to play along until he caught on. "I couldn't sleep," she said, trying to sound like James. "Those uncouth men snore like bears."

"Have you seen Sam?" Matthew asked.

"No," she replied, "and I'm beginning to worry."

"I offered to keep this watch on deck so I could spot her," Matthew confided. "But I am wearying of this duty fast."

"You know her, Matthew. She'll do whatever she pleases."

"I hope she comes before we set sail."

"Me too," Sam said. "She'll be madder than a wet wildcat if we leave without her."

"I'd not like to tangle with her," Matthew said.

"Neither would I," Samantha said. Overhead stars sparkled. "The Chickahominy Indians say that each star is the campfire of a dead warrior," Samantha said.

"That sounds like something Samantha would say . . ." Matthew began. He flashed the lantern light on her. "Well, dog my cats," he laughed. "Samantha Byrd, you'd fool your own mother."

She grinned and bowed. "James Byrd the Second at your service," she said.

Chapter 22

Samantha was going to explain her appearance, but Matthew put a finger to her lips.

"Tell me later," he whispered. "It is too risky here on deck."

She nodded.

"You will have to hide until I can talk to James. Samantha, sometimes you are more trouble than a family of skunks."

She punched him on the arm.

"Listen. Go down that hatch by the mast. Then go below that deck to the cargo hold. Hide among the barrels in the stern. Do you understand?"

"Yes," she whispered.

"Wait there until my watch is over at midnight. I'll come below and find you." He handed her his lantern.

Samantha climbed down through the hatch. In the gloom she could see the second hatch leading into the ship's hold. She peered down into the blackness. The smell of the bilge water rose like the breath of death. She wanted to pinch her nose closed, but she needed both hands to climb the ladder and hold the lantern. *I've smelled worse*, she told herself, thinking of a rotting horse carcass she had once seen. She climbed into the darkness.

When her feet touched the next deck, she pinched her nose. With her other hand, she held the lantern high as she found her way among the casks, barrels, and hogsheads stored below. Finding a wide space between two barrels, she sat down. She closed the lantern shutter. With her eyes useless in the pitch black, her ears sharpened. First she heard the gentle swish of Queen's Creek against the ship's sides. Timbers creaked. As the ship rolled, the contents of the barrels around her shifted. The meat in the cask she was leaning against sloshed back and forth. A dry rustling of claws clicking on the deck sent shivers down her spine.

Rats!

Samantha hugged her knees close to her chest. Closing her eyes, she wished for time to pass quickly. Her weariness slowly overcame her fear, and she slipped into sleep.

Matthew shook her awake. She almost screamed. His lantern blinded her for a moment. She rubbed the sleep from her eyes.

"I didn't mean to scare you," Matthew said.

"Makes no matter," she replied. "At least you're not a rat."

"Sam—" Matthew began.

Samantha cut him short. "Remember: I am James," she chided him.

"James," he began anew, "while on my watch, I think I solved our problem."

"How?"

"We set sail on the tide at dawn. You must remain here until I can talk with James."

"But—" she interrupted.

"Just listen, Sam . . . James," he insisted. "James must learn his duties today. Tonight he can tell them to you, and the following day you can trade places."

"I can't stay here in this stench for a whole day," she snapped. The thought of the rats made her skin crawl.

"Do you have any other ideas?" he hissed.

"No," she said. "But I'll think of one by morning."

Neither one of them said a word. Finally, Matthew broke the silence by handing her a wooden bucket and saying, "Here is bread, cheese, and water from the galley. It is not much, but it was all I could take without making the cook suspicious."

Samantha eagerly took the bucket and checked its contents. Half starved, she bit into the cheese.

Without another word Matthew disappeared into the darkness. She heard him climb the ladder. The ship's sounds returned.

Each creak and rustle seemed louder than before.

Samantha's eyes felt heavy, but she fought sleep. She had to plan. She couldn't last a whole day below decks, out of the sun and with the scurrying rats. She shined the lantern around her hideout. Pairs of red rat eyes flashed back. She wanted to throw something at them, but she couldn't afford to waste any food.

Try as she might, no plan came to Samantha. But sleep did.

The crash of the anchor chains woke her again. The *Cardinal* was getting under way.

Chapter 23

The *Cardinal* heeled slightly as her sails filled. Barrels shifted. Samantha shined the lantern to make sure those barrels near her were lashed down tightly. Some timbers were stacked against one side of the ship. She tested the rope holding them. It was tight.

The gentle swish of the water against the *Cardinal's* sides became a rush as the ship sliced through the water. *We must be on the James River*, Samantha calculated. She set the remaining cheese and bread on a barrel top and divided it into three equal portions: breakfast, dinner, and supper. Tonight, she and James would switch places.

After she had eaten, nature called. Samantha hadn't considered how she would relieve herself on the ship or even how sailors attended to this necessary task. Certainly some of their waste had trickled into the stinking bilge water sloshing just below her. She decided to use the bucket from Matthew as a chamber pot. Then she emptied the bucket into the bilge water below. She stored the bucket behind a cask, then sat upon a barrel and waited for Matthew.

An eternity seemed to pass before she heard steps on the ladder. In the dim light, she watched Matthew climb down into the hold. Someone trailed behind him.

James!

Matthew hurried to her. James followed, his hand cupped over his mouth. He spun away and emptied his stomach.

"He's seasick," Matthew whispered.

"I can see that," Samantha said. She hurried to help James, but he waved her away.

"Just hang my hammock and let me die," he said.

"Help me," Matthew said to Samantha. She turned from her brother.

"Shine the light around so we can find a place for his hammock."

Samantha opened the lantern cover and aimed the thin beam around the hold.

"Over here," Matthew told her.

She shined the light at the very stern of the ship.

"We can hang one end from this peg and the other end from this hook," Matthew said. He unrolled the hammock. They each fastened an end. James moaned and climbed into it.

"You will have to be quiet," Matthew said. "If we're discovered, Captain Black can still turn back."

"Let him," James sighed.

Samantha grabbed his arm hard. "No," she snapped. "We are following through with this, no matter what."

James yanked his arm out of her grasp and rolled onto his stomach. He retched again.

"Leave him," Matthew said. "We'll both be missed before long. Only the cook comes down here now that we're under way."

Samantha shined the light on James's heaving body and then turned away. There was nothing she could do for him until he got his sea legs. This was her chance to escape the hold. She felt sorry for James but . . .

The air on the main deck smelled as sweet as honey. She breathed in huge lungsful.

"You boys, there," someone yelled. "Get to your stations before my starter finds your backsides!" He snapped a short rope with a large knot on the end.

"That's Mr. Hands, the first mate," Matthew told her. "You'd best stand by the captain's door. That's where James was when I found him."

"What am I supposed to do?" Samantha asked.

"Whatever the captain orders. I'll talk with you at the noon mess."

Matthew hurried off toward the bow of the ship. He helped men tighten the ropes that kept the cannon from rolling.

Samantha reached the door just as it opened. Captain Black blinked in the bright sunlight and looked around.

"Feeling better, young Byrd?" he asked, his eyes lighting on Samantha. Without pausing for an answer he rambled on. "Time you learned your duties. I want me coffee at the sixth bell of morning watch. Steaming hot and black. Then make my bed and straighten my cabin. My breakfast will be on the table by eight bells."

Samantha did not move.

Captain Black eyed her. "You're wearing different clothes this morning, lad. Whether is it a long voyage or short, there's no need to change unless you are dead. Then you just wear your naturals! Har har!" he laughed at his own joke.

"Why some of these men haven't changed their clothes since we sailed last spring." He shook his head. "You are a green one," he chuckled. "No wonder your father wanted you to ship with me. When we steal the bone from the British bulldog, you'll grow up fast. You will be a man when we return."

"Aye, Captain," Samantha said. She fought down a chuckle herself. *I might grow up some, but I'll never be a man*, she thought.

"Now off with you. Me stomach growls." Captain Black climbed the short ladder to his quarterdeck, where he watched over the *Cardinal*.

Samantha turned. She remembered passing the galley on the way from the hold. She hurried down to it.

"Captain Black wants his coffee," she said to the cook, who was flipping griddlecakes. He pointed at a pot with his flapjack. "Best take the whole pot," he said. "What do they call you, son?"

"Sam. I mean James," Samantha said.

The cook looked at her. "Well Samjames. Hurry along. Don't keep Captain Black waiting."

"Thank you," Samantha said, picking up the pot.

"When you hear eight bells, get on back down here, Samjames. Captain's vittles be ready then." He returned to his cooking.

Samantha carried the pot to the foot of the ladder. Balancing the pot in one hand, she used the other hand to climb. *How will I carry a tray of food?* she wondered.

She knocked on the captain's door.

"Enter," he called.

Samantha placed the pot on a table. The *Cardinal* rolled and the pot began to slide. She grabbed it just before it reached the table's edge.

"Place it yon gimbals," the captain said.

She stood as stupid as a stick of wood. The captain pointed to a brass bracket on the cabin wall. Samantha placed the pot in the bracket, and it swiveled with the motion of the ship.

"I'll pour it myself today," Captain Black said.

He was reaching for the pot when a voice bellowed, "Sail ho!"

"Now the game begins," Captain Black said. He rushed to the deck.

Samantha dashed after him.

Chapter 24

Samantha could just see a white sail low on the horizon. The lookout called, "Three masts, sir."

"British or American?" the Captain asked.

"Can't rightly tell yet, sir," the sailor answered.

Captain Black turned to Samantha. "Lad, take this spyglass up to the lookout." He handed Samantha his wooden telescope. She took it, but her feet seemed to be made of lead. "Get a move on," Captain Black ordered, any hint of humor gone from his voice.

Gripping the spyglass in one hand, she grabbed the ratlines leading to the mast top with the other. Carefully, she put one foot on the ropes.

She had not climbed 10 feet when she realized that she needed both hands to carry on. She tucked the telescope into her breeches. As she did, she made the mistake of looking down. She hadn't climbed far, but she was already too high to suit her fancy. She looked up. The maintop appeared as high as a 200-year-old oak.

A voice whispered at her shoulder. "Sam. Follow me. Don't look down." It was Matthew.

She waited until he climbed past, then she followed. She put her feet exactly where he put his. He makes it look so easy, she thought. But then, he had sailed on a tall ship before.

Ages seemed to pass before they neared the lookout's platform. She was tempted to look down, but she didn't. Even from where she was, she could feel the swaying of the mast as the *Cardinal* rolled first to one side, then the other.

Her arms ached. Her soles felt on fire. Still she climbed. All at once, Matthew's feet dangled directly above her head. She looked at him. He was swinging outward, pulling himself the last few feet with just his arms. He said over his shoulder, "Climb through the lubber's hole."

She didn't argue. She struggled through the hole and collapsed on the platform.

The lookout snatched the glass from her waist. "Took your sweet time, lad," he growled. He trained the spyglass on the ship. Samantha, holding onto a rope, pulled herself up.

She gasped in amazement. A whole new world spread below her. The broad James River rolled immensely before her. She looked downstream, almost to Newport it seemed. Fishing skiffs the size of the *Fish Hawk* looked like toy boats as they skimmed across the brown water.

"She's British," the lookout yelled to the deck below. "I can make out her flag. She's spotted us, sir. She's giving chase!"

"All hands on deck!" bellowed Captain Black. Samantha took a quick look down. It was if someone had kicked open an anthill. Men scurried in all directions.

"Down you both go," the lookout ordered.

Reluctantly, Samantha followed Matthew back down the ratlines. *I will climb aloft again—faster,* she promised herself.

Samantha and Matthew joined the rest of the crew gathered before the quarterdeck. All eyes were on Captain Black.

"Lads, I know you joined me to capture prizes. Appears we have a warship dogging our heels. We can't outgun her, so we will have to outrun her." A groan rippled through the crew. "I promised you a prize, and a prize we will take. You all know that if we're captured, you will be pressed into His Majesty's service for the rest of your lives." His steely gaze swept over the men. "Let's show 'em our heels. Mr. Hands, put on all the sail she can take."

Mr. Hands snapped his starter. "You heard the captain," he shouted.

The men scattered, each to do his duty. There was no grumbling now, not with a British warship after them.

Samantha couldn't hide her disappointment. She wanted to fight. She wanted to get Henry back. She didn't want to run like some cowardly dog. But what if they themselves were captured? After all, they had only two cannons.

Captain Black called her. "Fetch me other glass from me cabin," he said. "And be quick about it."

When Samantha returned to the deck, some sailors had swarmed into the rigging and had unfurled a small topsail. Others had raised two more jibs. With five sails filled, the *Cardinal* kicked up her heels like a playful colt and galloped through the water.

Captain Black chuckled to himself. "You think we're the fox and you the hounds," he said out loud to the British ship. "You are right in that. But this fox knows a few tricks that you bulldogs have never seen. "Throw over the sea anchor," Captain Black ordered.

Chapter 25

Samantha watched five sailors carry an old sail past the captain. A row of cannonballs hung from it. The sailors tied two corners of the sail to the ship and dropped the sail into the water. The *Cardinal* immediately slowed.

Disappointment etched Samantha's face. "What are you doing?" she cried out.

Captain Black's look withered her and she shrunk back. Matthew grabbed her elbow and steered her away. "You fool," he hissed. "Never, and I mean never, question the captain."

"But we're slowing down. We'll get captured."

"Look up," Matthew told her. She gazed at the full set of sails still filled with wind. Even with the wind pushing them, the *Cardinal* slowed even more.

"Captain Black has a trick up his sleeve," he said. "To

the British ship, we look like we are trying to escape using all the sails we can."

Samantha caught on. "But with that sail acting like an anchor we are actually slowing down so she can catch up with us. But why?"

"I suspect that Captain Black has a surprise for them," Matthew said.

Samantha wondered what kind of surprise a ship carrying two guns could have for a warship. Time would tell.

The sails of the British ship grew larger and larger. Before long, Samantha could see individual men along the railing. They were rolling out a row of six cannons. The cannons' black snouts looked vicious.

A puff of smoke rose from one cannon. A boom followed like thunder after lightning. The cannonball splashed into the water ahead of the *Cardinal*.

"Loose the sails," Captain Black ordered. "Cut loose the sea anchor." He turned to Samantha, "And you keep your mouth shut."

Samantha shrank back as the orders were followed.

Two sailors chopped the ropes holding the sea anchor. Weighted by the cannonballs, it sank. The *Cardinal* gradually slowed, then stopped, as the wind spilled from her sails.

"Ahoy there," called a sailor from the British ship. "Stand to and prepare for boarding."

"Aye," Captain Black called through his speaking trumpet. In a voice only the *Cardinal's* crew heard, he said,

"Now lads, you know the routine." Ten heads nodded, even Samantha's.

Then she remembered James down below in the hold. She pinched Matthew and whispered, "What about James?"

Matthew grimaced, for he had forgotten James too.

"Should I go below and make certain everything is secured?" Matthew asked Captain Black.

"Aye, Matthew. And take James with you. Keep him with you until the British have gone."

"Aye-aye, sir," Matthew said, pulling Samantha with him toward the hatch.

He grabbed a lantern and stopped to light it at the galley stove. Samantha followed wordlessly as they climbed down into the hold.

James was where they had left him, swinging miserably in his hammock.

"Get up, James," Matthew said.

"Leave me alone," he growled.

"We can't," Matthew told him. "We've been stopped by a British ship. They will search the hold."

"I don't care," he moaned. "Let them capture me and put me back on dry land."

"Well, we care," Samantha said. She grabbed the edge of the hammock and flipped him out. In the dim light she saw the tears in his eyes. Instead of feeling sorry for him, she shook him. "Now listen, you blockhead," she snarled.

"Calm down, Sam," Matthew said.

"We'll be discovered if we don't do something fast," she

snapped at him.

Matthew rubbed his eyes. "You are right," he said. "But what can we do?"

"Where can I hide?" Samantha asked.

"You?" Matthew questioned.

"Yes, me. Only one of us can be here when they come below." An idea dawned on her and made her stomach flip. "Is there a way down into the bilge?"

"Yes, but why?"

"I will hide there and James can be himself."

"I'm too sick," he whimpered.

"You will be sicker when Captain Black finds out our trick," Samantha said. "Or would you rather go down into the bilge?"

James looked as if he was going to get sick again.

"This way," Matthew said. He led them to a small hatch well past the stack of logs. "They use this hatch to clean the bilge."

"Probably never been opened," Samantha quipped. She bent down and lifted the heavy hatch cover. A blast of stench hit her. Both boys stepped back. "Smells worse than 10 skunks trapped in a tobacco shed," she choked out.

Samantha lowered herself down into the darkness. Her feet felt a wooden knee supporting the ship's side. She hunched herself down upon it. Already she could hear footsteps approaching the ladder to the hold.

"Don't leave me down here a second too long," she ordered.

"I won't," Matthew promised, gagging as he dropped the hatch down.

Never before had Samantha experienced anything so totally black. There was not one glimmer of light in any direction. She closed her eyes and concentrated on taking short, shallow breaths. Overhead she heard footsteps crossing the deck, stopping here and there. Muffled voices drifted her way, but she could not make out a word. Finally the footsteps faded. When the hatch cover opened she scrambled out, gasping for breath. Firm arms gripped her. Not Matthew's. Not James's.

She looked right into Captain Black's face.

Chapter 26

"Just as I thought," Captain Black said. "When I saw that the bilge cover had been moved, I knew there was a stowaway in the bilge."

Matthew and James stood behind him.

"Methinks there is some explaining to do," Captain Black said. "We'd best settle this in my cabin."

Samantha wanted to pull Matthew aside and ask what had happened with the British, but she held her tongue. She was already in enough trouble. Trouble follows me like a hungry puppy, she thought. If only I hadn't been discovered, we could find Henry.

Captain Black sat in his chair. The three cousins stood before him.

"Who is to tell this tale?" the captain asked.

Matthew and James looked at Samantha.

"I will," she said. "We were trying to help rescue Henry and I wanted to sail with you so James and I dressed alike so I could and if only James hadn't gotten sick we—"

"Whoa," Captain Black said, holding up his hand. "You are galloping like a runaway horse."

Samantha paused and took a deep breath before slowly explaining the whole story to Captain Black.

When she finished, he broke into a grin. "If you don't beat all," he chuckled. "Samantha, I mean Sam Byrd, you have more gumption than most lads your age." He stroked his salt-and-pepper beard and continued, "We're too far to turn back. If my plans work out, I'll be needing all the men I can muster. If the men don't know you're a girl, I can sign you on as another hand, say as James's twin brother."

"When you capture British ships?" Samantha burst out.

Captain Black rocketed up from his chair. "How do you know that?" he barked.

"I overheard you talking with Papa and Uncle John."

Captain Black stroked his beard while he thought. He sat back down. "Since you will be part of the crew now, I'd best tell you all," he said. "I do indeed have a letter of marque giving me permission to capture British ships. I also possess a letter from Lord Dunmore giving me permission to supply his ships and transport materials and Loyalists for him."

"You can't do that!" Samantha said.

Captain Black fixed her with a stern stare. Samantha was quiet.

"I am just as loyal to Virginia as your Pa and your uncle. We're all Sons of Liberty aboard this ship. With Dunmore thinking me loyal to the King, I can further our cause at his expense."

"But how?" Samantha asked.

"Like I just did fooling the *Otter*'s lieutenant," he explained.

"How?" Samantha asked.

"When they boarded us, I showed their lieutenant me letter from Dunmore giving me permission to supply him. The letter also protects me crew from being pressed into the British Navy. Just like in England, the crews of supply ships can't be taken from their ships. I showed him the casks of beef we were carrying for Dunmore, and the timbers for firewood. Seems few Loyalists will venture far from Newport for food or wood because our militia pesters them when they do."

"But how can you take supplies to Dunmore?" Samantha asked.

"I'm not," Captain Black told her. "It is a ruse to allow me to slip past Newport so we can prowl the Chesapeake for our quarry . . . real British supply ships. If we stayed up the James, we'd be trapped like rats."

Samantha shivered at the mention of those beady-eyed pests.

"Enough jabbering," Captain Black said. "You now know what the rest of the crew knows. Are you willing to sign on?"

"Yes, sir," Samantha said.

Captain Black passed a book over to her. He opened it and said, "Put your mark there."

Samantha took up his quill pen and signed "Sam Byrd" right under James's signature.

"Now back to your duties . . . lads," Captain Black ordered. He shook his head. "Usually I am the one playing tricks, but Samantha, I mean Sam, you pulled one over on me. I like that."

The three rushed from the cabin into the bright September sun. Far astern, the *Otter* continued west up the James while the *Cardinal* sailed east toward Newport. James ran to the railing and retched.

"Now tell me what else happened while I was hiding in the bilge," Samantha demanded.

"After I left you, the British boarded us. Captain Black's plan was to make us look like we weren't sure if the *Otter* was really a British ship or one of ours. That's why he had the sea anchor slowing us down. Without it we can outrun any ship in the Royal Navy. But with the anchor, we could look like we were trying to escape when we really weren't."

"Then what?"

"Captain Black showed his letter from Dunmore and led the lieutenant around the ship. Satisfied that we were what we said we were, he let us go. Now we can sail past Newport and begin capturing ships!"

"The one Henry is on, I hope," Samantha said.

Captain Black opened his door and called, "Sam Byrd,

fetch me some hot coffee. This pot has gone cold. And send the carpenter to me."

Samantha quickly completed her errands and helped James below to his hammock. When she returned to the deck, the carpenter and his mate were cutting out sections of the railing.

"Mr. Hands, bring out the quakers," Captain Black ordered.

"Step lively, lads," Mr. Hands yelled. He snapped his starter to back up his words.

Samantha remained near Captain Black, watching the activity. The sailors brought eight logs up from the hold. They rolled them into the places where the railings had been cut. When the logs were fastened, the sailors painted them black.

All at once Samantha understood. The "quakers" were fake cannons, made to fool an enemy ship into thinking they were real. Since most merchant ships carried only one or two cannons at the most, the *Cardinal* would appear heavily armed. Any ship they chased might surrender rather than fight.

"Fine work, men," Captain Black said when they had finished. "Now we carry 10 cannons. And paint over the name *Cardinal*. We are the *Liberty* of the Navy of the Colony of Virginia!"

"Three cheers for the *Liberty*!" yelled Mr. Hands.

"Huzzah! Huzzah! Huzzah!" shouted the crew. Samantha cheered the loudest.

Chapter 27

As the crew settled into a routine, the days passed quickly. The *Liberty* slipped past Newport without problems. Now she cruised the open waters of the Chesapeake Bay. James got his sea legs and could eat. He shared the cabin boy duties with Samantha. They told the other sailors that she was his twin brother Sam.

Matthew warned Samantha and James that sailors were superstitious about having a woman aboard, for she would bring bad luck.

One sailor was always on lookout high up the mast. When not on duty, Samantha and Matthew often climbed up to join him. The swaying of the mast was too much for James, so he kept to the deck.

Samantha especially enjoyed the view from the mast. She felt as if she could reach up and touch the flocks of white clouds sailing over them. Like everyone aboard, she watched for sails on the horizon.

A week passed without sighting even one. When she asked Mr. Hands about this, he told her that most merchant ships were huddled near Newport under the protection of Lord Dunmore. However, there were supply ships coming from England, hoping to reach America before the fall storms came in full force. Having been caught in that hurricane, Samantha understood their worry.

Tory ships from Maryland and Virginia were also still trading. Mr. Hands explained that some merchant ships were being used to house Tories until they could sail home to England. She wished that Thomas Wormley was on one. How would they ever find Henry if they never saw any ships?

As each day ended Samantha grew more discouraged about rescuing Henry. She talked with Matthew about it. But like everyone else, he had no idea when they might meet a ship—or even if they could capture a ship, much less the one with Henry aboard.

"Even if we do capture a ship," Samantha said. "What will we do with it?"

"The sailors on my watch told me that the captain plans to capture a small ship and use the cannons from it to add to ours. When we have enough real guns, we will attack a larger ship. He will take command of the captured ship and place Mr. Hands in command of the *Liberty*. The ships we capture will be sold as prizes in Yorktown."

Ten days after they had sailed from Burleigh's Landing, the lookout called, "Sail ho!" Everyone rushed to the deck, gazing in the direction that the sailor was pointing. Samantha could just make out a small dot of sail on the horizon.

"Run up the British flag," Captain Black ordered. "Maybe she'll give in without a fight."

"Not fight!" Samantha said to Matthew.

Matthew looked at her in surprise. "You are the one who preaches 'thou shalt not kill,'" he said.

Samantha blushed, her skin matching her red hair. In her excitement she had forgotten that when they went into battle, people would be hurt—even killed.

"Captain Black is as wily as fox," she said. "Maybe we can take that ship without wasting a shot."

"Especially as we have only enough gunpowder for 10 rounds for each cannon," Matthew informed her.

How will we ever win a war with England with so few supplies? Samantha wondered. Then she answered her own question: *By capturing supplies from the British bulldog!*

The sailor aloft called down, "She's seen us, sir, and is showing us her heels."

"Mr. Hands," said Captain Black, "order hands aloft. Let loose all the sail we can carry. We are in the chase."

Men scurried up the ratlines and unfurled every sail. With the wind at her stern, the *Liberty*'s sails bulged, and she pushed her after her quarry. Before long, Samantha saw more of the other ship's sails as the *Liberty* closed the distance between them.

Samantha was feeling the same thrill of excitement that she felt when she trailed a deer. The other ship was trying to reach the safety of Newport just as a deer seeks shelter in the forest. But if the *Liberty* were fast enough, they would catch the British ship before it reached safety.

The wind held, and the *Liberty* gained rapidly on the foe. Soon Samantha could see the crew of the ship standing by its two cannons. She could read the ship's name: *Falcon*.

"She's heavy with goods," Matthew said. "She can't fly like a falcon. She wallows like a pig in mud."

"Fire a warning shot, Mr. Hands," ordered Captain Black.

The gun crew stepped back as Mr. Hands applied his match to the cannon's wick. The powder flashed. The cannon roared. The wind cleared the smoke and Samantha saw the shot fall just off the other ship's bow.

The rest of the crew stood by the quakers and pretended to load them.

The *Falcon* dropped her sails and hove to. She struck her colors, lowering her British flag.

"Mr. Hands, prepare a boarding party. She is ours."

Mr. Hands's eyes roamed the crew. "O'Dell, Woods, Hancock, Byrd. Come with me."

Samantha stood stock-still. Which Byrd?

Mr. Hands glared at her. "Step lively, Sam Byrd, or I'll choose another."

Samantha dashed across the deck and joined the others in lowering the gig. She scrambled down the side of the

Liberty and into the small boat. She looked up to see Matthew hauling down the *Liberty*'s false British flag and raising Virginia's rattlesnake flag in its place.

"Pull hearty, me lads," Mr. Hands ordered. "We just plucked a plump goose."

Samantha grabbed an oar and dug it into the water. The crew found its rhythm, and the gig skimmed across to the other ship. Samantha was glad she knew how to row.

The *Falcon* was twice the size of the *Liberty*. Samantha imagined what could be in her hold. James's share of the prize money might be enough for him to go to William and Mary. If only she had a share too. Then Papa could buy the land he wanted. If only.

She didn't even dare hope that Henry was aboard.

Samantha was the last to board the *Falcon*. She scanned the deck for Henry. He wasn't there.

With a pistol in each hand, Mr. Hands took command of the *Falcon* while her crew stood at the railings. Most of the men wore expressions of gloomy hostility. Three, however, grinned from ear to ear.

"Are any of you men Americans?" Mr. Hands called out.

"Aye, sir," one of the smiling men announced. "We three were pressed off the *Hornet* last spring."

"Where might you hail from?" asked Mr. Hands.

"Boston," he said.

"Step forward, men," Mr. Hands ordered.

They moved quickly to join the crew from the *Cardinal*.

"The *Falcon* now belongs to the Colony of Virginia,"

Mr. Hands said. "Any of you who wish to join us, step this way. The rest will be confined below deck until we can put you ashore."

"You thieving American dog," growled one the *Falcon*'s crew. "I'll see you in Hades before I join you."

"Byrd, place him in irons," Mr. Hands ordered. He thrust a set of handcuffs at Samantha. She took the cuffs and walked toward the man. He glared at her as if she might be a tidbit for breakfast. *What if he doesn't let me cuff him?* she wondered. Then she heard the click of the triggers on Mr. Hands's pistols.

With a look that would have melted steel, the man held out his wrists to her. She snapped the cuffs on him and stepped quickly out of his reach.

"Anyone else?" Mr. Hands asked. Without a word, the *Falcon*'s crew climbed down the ladder. Mr. Hands dropped the cover over the hatch and padlocked it.

"Byrd. Woods. Row the *Falcon*'s captain to the *Liberty*, where he will be Captain Black's guest."

The captured captain slammed his hat down on his head. He climbed into the gig and glowered as they rowed him to the *Liberty*. His outrage erupted fully when he saw that all but two of the *Liberty*'s cannons were wood. "You will hang for this," he snarled. His gaze fell on the members of the *Liberty*'s crew as if he were memorizing their faces.

Samantha rubbed her neck. A rope would be ever so much tighter than her corset.

Chapter 28

Captain Black sent three of the *Liberty*'s crew to join Mr. Hands on the *Falcon*. He ordered them to sail to Yorktown and sell the *Falcon* as a prize. The *Liberty*, in need of supplies, would join her in a week.

Before the *Falcon* departed, her two cannons were swung aboard the *Liberty*. They replaced two of the quakers. Five barrels of powder and one hundred cannonballs were also brought aboard the *Liberty*.

With eight of *Liberty*'s crew now on the *Falcon*, Samantha, James, and Matthew had extra duties. Because she was so good at climbing, Samantha worked raising and lowering the sails. Matthew was on her watch. James became the sole cabin boy. Everything he learned from Captain Black he passed on to Samantha.

Samantha's true identity still remained a secret. The

sailors treated her like a lad. She joined in the fun, but she was more serious than ever before in her life. Each day her frustration grew at her inability to do anything to help Henry. She was used to taking charge, being in command. On the *Liberty* she had no choice but to follow the rules of the ship and the orders of Captain Black.

"I wish I could go ashore to hunt," Samantha announced one noon. She poked at a bit of dried beef on her plate. "Fresh skunk would be better than this."

An older sailor grinned toothlessly. "Laddie, this is nothing. When I sailed aboard the *Rose*, we ate nothing but horsemeat and biscuits for three months. The biscuits were more weevil than wheat. Had to crack 'em against the table till all of the weevils fell out. Me teeth, they fell out from the scurvy." He chomped his gums together.

"But if Captain Black lets me ashore, I can shoot a deer and we'll have fresh meat."

"Sam, you know he doesn't dare let us leave unless we have to. You never can tell when one of Dunmore's ships might try to flee."

That afternoon, when she wasn't on duty, Samantha climbed the mast to enjoy the view. The sailor aloft greeted her and left her to her thoughts. The *Liberty* plunged through the bay like a porpoise. Samantha scanned the horizon.

Suddenly she rubbed her eyes. Far to the west, a tiny sail moved along. At first she wasn't sure if it was a sail or a cloud. She couldn't make out a ship at first, but as she watched, another sail came into view.

"Look!" she yelled.

The sailor followed her finger. "Good eyes, Sam," he complimented her. "Looks like one of Dunmore's flock is venturing forth."

"Sail ahoy!" he shouted to the deck. "Off our port bow."

Samantha kept her eyes on the sail, willing it to come closer. A British flag fluttered from the ship's mast.

Breathless, Matthew joined them, the captain's telescope in his hand. He passed it to the sailor, who trained it on the sails.

"She hasn't seen us yet," he whispered, almost as if the ship could hear him. "But she will soon enough."

The hot sun burned down, but neither Samantha nor Matthew wanted to leave the mast. Reluctantly, they did when Captain Black ordered all hands on deck. By then they had cut their distance to the ship by half.

I hope Henry is aboard, Samantha said to herself as they climbed down.

For a long time, Captain Black stared at the ship. "Men," he said. "We'll take another prize if the wind holds out. Prepare for action." The men scurried to their posts. "Break out the muskets and small arms. This ship will be putting up a fight. Both you Byrds come with me," he ordered.

Samantha and James followed him below. He unlocked the cabinet holding the guns and powder. He handed two muskets to Samantha. "Take these up on deck and give them to Mr. Walker," he ordered. The cool musket barrels felt good in Samantha's hands. She longed to aim one. James, carrying the powder and shot, poked her to hurry up.

The *Liberty's* four cannons had been loaded and rolled out. Three men stood at each gun ready to fire and reload.

Samantha gave the muskets to Mr. Walker, wishing she had one too. "Thou shalt not kill," Mama's words echoed in her ears.

Samantha hurried below to fetch more muskets. James followed.

When Samantha returned to the deck, she saw that they had gotten even closer to the ship.

Sam and James returned for a third trip when Mr. Walker said, "James, take this bucket of powder up to the first cannon. And be fast about it. You will be the powder monkey during the fight. If you are wounded, then your brother can take over." With that, he handed the bucket to Sam. Rather than argue that she was really Sam, not James, she took it and climbed carefully to the deck. She dare not spill a grain of the precious powder.

She placed the bucket by the first cannon and dashed for more. She didn't even glance at the other ship until she had carried up a powder bucket for each gun.

"Stand back, lads," a sailor shouted. He raised his match in anticipation of Captain Black's order to fire.

The order came promptly. The sailor touched the match to the wick. The powder sputtered. The cannon crashed against its ropes as it fired. Smoke hung in the air, then cleared. All eyes were on the other ship. The shot plunged into the water far behind her.

Samantha saw smoke rise from a cannon mounted on the opposing ship's stern. She ducked as the shot whistled through the rigging. It cut a rope, which fell to the deck like a dead snake.

"Fire as you bear," Captain Black ordered. As the *Liberty* closed the gap between the two ships, her second cannon fired. Then her third. The first was already reloaded, and her crew fired it. A cheer went up as the cannonball struck home, hitting the ship's quarterdeck.

"More powder," someone yelled. Samantha grabbed an empty bucket and went below. She had just reached the top of the ladder when the world seemed to explode. A shower of splinters flew through air like a horde of hornets. A sailor cried out. Samantha looked his way. A jagged piece of oak stabbed through his arm like a knife. She fought down a gag.

She looked for James and Matthew. James was loading muskets and passing them to sailors lining the railing. Several had climbed aloft, their powder horns and shot pouches dangling.

Where was Matthew? She ran up the deck, careful not to slip on the blood oozing from another wounded sailor.

A cannonball whizzed overhead, cutting through the jib. The sail split. The *Liberty* bucked now that she had lost such an important sail. Without being ordered, sailors cut the whipping sail loose.

"Where is Matthew?" she shouted at a sailor. He pointed to a heap huddled against the far side of the ship.

Matthew lay still, blood from a wound spreading in a red pool around him.

Matthew!

Dead!

Rage burst through Samantha like a spark through gunpowder. She snatched a musket from a wounded man. Running to the railing, she picked out her target: a tall man struggling to steer the enemy ship. His face was turned away, but she had a clear shot at him. She drew a deep breath.

"Thou shalt not kill" echoed in her head.

"An eye for an eye, Mama," Samantha whispered. "They killed Matthew. One of them will die too." She squeezed the trigger.

The man at the wheel turned just as the powder flashed.

Henry's eyes locked with hers as he grasped his chest.

Chapter 29

Samantha's world spun. She couldn't have shot Henry. Only in her overwhelming anger did she consider shooting anyone. But Henry?

Samantha slumped to the deck. She threw the musket away. She would never touch another gun for as long as she lived.

Henry.

Maybe she had only wounded him. No, she had aimed for his heart. At this distance she could not miss. She had seen him collapse, clutching his chest.

I'll die too, she decided. *Another eye for an eye. My life for his life.*

Samantha stood and faced the enemy ship. She gasped in surprise. The *Liberty* was only a few feet away from the other ship, her pointed bowsprit already tangled in the ship's rigging. With a grinding crash, the two ships smashed together. Ropes snapped. Wood cracked. Men cried out.

"Boarders away," screamed Captain Black. Dazed, Samantha watched as the *Liberty*'s crew leaped onto the decks of the other boat. Swords and knives clashed. Pistols popped. Men yelled in anger and agony.

Suddenly silence fell. Samantha, rooted at the railing, watched as the enemy's flag dropped. She didn't cheer with the others when the *Liberty*'s flag climbed the ship's mast.

Tears refused to come. She just slumped against the railing.

"Sam, are you hurt?" It was James, his face smeared black with gunpowder. One eyebrow had been singed off. He called to her from the other ship.

"I killed Henry," she managed to croak. Her throat was as dry as a bone. "I killed Henry," she repeated.

"Henry?" James asked. "What do you mean?" James climbed over the ship's side to her.

"They killed Matthew. So I killed one of them too. An eye for eye."

James shook her. "Sam, Matthew is only wounded in the leg. I talked with him. He fainted at the sight of his own blood. But don't tell anyone."

His words came to her as if through a fog and from a long distance away. Matthew was only wounded, not dead. And she had killed Henry in revenge!

"We must fetch Henry so we can bury him properly," she snapped.

James held out a hand to help her across, but she pushed it away. She would do this herself, as she did everything else.

If only I had never learned to shoot, she thought.

The deck of the other ship was littered with splintered wood, ripped sails, and cut ropes. Everywhere, wounded men moaned. Others lay silent, never to speak again.

She stepped around the clutter and ignored the injured. She made for the wheel. Her heart stopped when she saw Henry. She recognized his hunting shirt now. Why hadn't she noticed it before? Her anger had blazed too high for reason.

Samantha cradled Henry's head in her lap. Blood from his wound stained her breeches. "Why did I pull the trigger?" she howled as the tears finally burst forth.

"Because you are a hunter," came a whisper.

Henry had spoken. The fog in her head cleared.

"You . . . you . . . you are alive?" she asked.

"No thanks to you," Henry said. "I won't be for long if you don't stop drowning me with your tears."

"But I shot you," she said.

"Yes, you did. Bad shot as you are, you only wounded me," Henry said. "The ball passed through my shoulder. Still, it hurts worse than a mule kick. Help me stand."

Samantha gripped Henry under his arms. James helped too. Together they got him on his feet.

"Now get me aboard your ship so my feet don't have to tread this Tory deck any longer."

They helped Henry to the *Liberty*'s deck.

"Let me check your wound," James said.

"It's nothing but a flesh wound," Henry told him.

"Hush, Henry, and do as I say," James commanded.

"Aye, brother," he said, impressed with the sudden authority in James's voice.

James took his clasp knife and cut Henry's shirt. Blood poured from a hole in his right shoulder. Ripping apart the shirt, James dabbed away the blood. Pressing the rag to the wound, he held it there until the bleeding stopped.

"Fetch some water, Sam," James ordered. She returned with a flask and held it to Henry's mouth. He drank deeply.

"Now if you could only heal my head as easily," Henry said.

Samantha noticed a gash on Henry's head. "You were wounded twice?" she asked.

"No, only once. I hit my head against the wheel when I fell."

Samantha ripped a piece off her shirt. Mama would be furious, she thought. She poured water onto the cloth and bathed the wound.

Henry winced at her touch. "Gentle. Sam, you have the hands of a blacksmith."

More tears began trickling down Samantha's face. She let them flow.

"Are you hurt?" Henry asked.

"No, you silly oaf. I am crying with happiness. You are alive."

The day passed in a blur. Samantha stayed with Henry,

feeding him soup and forcing him to drink plenty of water. James helped her when he could, but he was busy tending the wounds of other injured men.

Henry smiled at him. "They might make a doctor out of you yet at William and Mary."

James grinned. "With my share of the prize money, Papa will allow me to go."

"I will set him straight if he doesn't," Henry assured James.

As the *Liberty* limped to Yorktown with the other ship in tow, Henry told Samantha all that had befallen him since his capture. "I was looking for you, thinking you had sailed into the river and had been caught by the storm. Instead, I was caught by the *Otter*'s tender. They pressed me into duty on two ships anchored at Newport. I kept trying to escape, so they put me on the *Wye* to get me away from shore. We were sailing to Maryland to get reinforcements. Only, your *Liberty* happened along to give me back my liberty."

"How is that you were at the wheel when we attacked?" she asked.

"The bosun had been downed. I grabbed the ship's wheel and turned her into your path."

Matthew laughed. "That you did. Captain Black hadn't planned on boarding her so quickly."

James had cleaned and bound Matthew's leg. Matthew limped slightly, but the wound would heal nicely.

They docked the following day at sunset. Men, women, and children crowded the wharf to cheer as the

Liberty's crew landed. Henry was carried on a litter to the Elkhorn Tavern. After they helped him upstairs to rest, Samantha, James, and Matthew wolfed down steaming bowls of oyster stew.

Samantha had just broken off a piece of bread when her hand stopped. At a nearby table, staring at her, sat Thomas Wormley. His companion had a dirty brown bloodstain on his shirt. It was in the exact spot that Henry had shot the man who had stolen the *Fish Hawk*.

Samantha's joy disappeared in an instant.

Chapter 30

Thomas Wormley glared at them.

Samantha poked James. "There's Wormley and his friend."

James and Matthew looked in their direction. Wormley curled a lip in a snarl and started to stand up. Behind him, Captain Black clasped a hand on his shoulder. "You'd best sit back down," he said, pushing Wormley onto the bench.

Wormley tried to shrug off his hand.

"Those lads are mates on my ship," Captain Black said. "Leave them be."

"But . . . their . . . father . . . " Wormley stammered.

"Their father is part owner of the *Liberty*," Captain Black said. "And from what I just heard, he is part owner of your plantation."

Samantha leapt to her feet. "What did you say, Captain?"

"It appears Mr. Wormley is on his way to England to join his Tory friends. He sold his plantation."

"But I never sold any land to William Byrd. I'd die sooner than sell to him."

"Mr. Byrd has plumb outsmarted you," Captain Black explained. "You sold the land to Mr. Oxford, who in turn sold the finest 300 acres to Mr. Byrd."

"How do you know?" Wormley asked.

"Why, from Mr. William Byrd himself."

Samantha's mouth fell open as Papa stood. She had not recognized him, sitting with his back turned.

Samantha ran to Papa and hugged him. He pried her loose. "Why, James. It is unmanly to hug your father in public."

"Papa, don't you recognize me? I'm Sam . . . Samantha!"

Papa pulled her close. "I know," he whispered. "Lord, how I know."

"But how did you know we would be here?" she asked.

"Captain Black sent word to me with Mr. Hands from the *Falcon*."

"Do you know that Henry is back?" she asked.

"Yes, Samantha, I know that too. And how you nearly killed him trying to rescue him. I haven't seen him yet, as he needs his rest. The morning will be soon enough."

Their attention was diverted by a scene at the door. "Out you go," ordered the innkeeper. "I serve no Tories here."

Thomas Wormley looked as if he was going to say
something to the innkeeper but thought the better of it.
He had no allies at this inn. He turned his hatred on Papa.
"When I inform Lord North of this outrage, you'll hang
for this, Byrd."

He shut his mouth as a pewter mug flew past his head.
Laughter burst from a group across the room. One man
held a plate, his arm cocked to throw. Mr. Wormley and
his companion slammed the door as the plate hit it.

"Enough, lads," shouted the innkeeper. "He won't be
back."

"How did you get the money to buy Mr. Wormley's
land?" Samantha asked as they sat back down.

"Mr. Oxford loaned it me. With my shares and James's
share of the prize money from the *Falcon*, I almost had
enough. But your share will provide the remainder, plus
enough left over to send James to William and Mary."

"My share?"

Captain Black erupted into laughter behind her. "Sam.
I mean Samantha. My conscience would not rest if you
did not receive your share of the prize. After all, you
crewed as well as any lad and helped capture the enemy."

Samantha had so many questions to ask to Papa. She
felt like a dam holding back a spring flood and ready to
burst. "How is Mama? Did she read my note? How did
she feel about James and me being gone? Was she worried?
Will she forgive us?"

Papa put a finger to her mouth. "Come, Samantha,"
he said. "Young ladies are not allowed in taverns."

"But, Papa," she began. "I'm not . . . " She hesitated. "I

mean . . . " She was so confused. She had played the boy. But after what she saw of killing, did she still wish to?

If only there was no war.

If only her life had stayed the way it was, so she could roam the woods and streams.

If only.

The 13 Original Colonies

Signing the Declaration of Independence

The Declaration of Independence

Proclamation of the Earl of Dunmore

By his Excellency the Right Honorable JOHN Earl of
DUNMORE, His MAJESTY's Lieutenant and Governor General
of the Colony and Dominion of VIRGINIA, and Vice Admiral of
the same.

A PROCLAMATION.

AS I have ever entertained Hopes that an
Accommodation might have taken Place between GREAT-
BRITAIN and this colony, without being compelled by my
Duty to this most disagreeable but now absolutely
necessary Step, rendered so by a Body of armed Men
unlawfully assembled, bring on His MAJESTY's Tenders,
and the formation of an Army, and that Army now on
their March to attack His MAJESTY's troops and destroy
the well disposed Subjects of this Colony. To defeat such
unreasonable Purposes, and that all such Traitors, and
their Abetters, may be brought to Justice, and that the
Peace, and good Order of this Colony may be again
restored, which the ordinary Course of the Civil Law is
unable to effect; I have thought fit to issue this my
Proclamation, hereby declaring, that until the aforesaid
good Purposes can be obtained, I do in Virtue of the
Power and Authority to ME given, by His MAJESTY,
determine to execute Martial Law, and cause the same to
be executed throughout this Colony: and to the end that
Peace and good Order may the sooner be effected, I do
require every Person capable of bearing Arms, to resort to

His MAJESTY's STANDARD, or be looked upon as Traitors to His MAJESTY's Crown and Government, and thereby become liable to the Penalty the Law inflicts upon such Offences; such as forfeiture of Life, confiscation of lands, &cc. &cc. And I do hereby further declare all indentured Servants, Negroes, or others, (appertaining to Rebels,) free that are able and willing to bear Arms, they joining His MAJESTY's Troops as soon as may be, for the more speedily reducing this Colony to a proper Sense of their Duty, to His MAJESTY's Crown and Dignity. I do further order, and require, all his MAJESTY's Leige Subjects, to retain their Quitrents, or any other Taxes due or that may become due, in their own Custody, till such Time as Peace may be again restored to this at present most unhappy Country, or demanded of them for their former salutary Purposes, by Officers properly authorised to receive the same.

GIVEN under my Hand on board the Ship WILLIAM, off NORFOLK, the 7th Day of NOVEMBER, in the SIXTEENTH Year of His MAJESTY's Reign.

DUNMORE.
(GOD save the KING.)